100 THINGS TO DO IN FAYETTEVILLE NORTH CAROLINA BEFORE YOU DIE

Iron Mike, courtesy of DistiNCtly Fayetteville

100 THINGS TO DO IN FAYETTEVILLE NORTH CAROLINA BEFORE YOU DIE

MELODY FOOTE

Copyright © 2023 by Reedy Press, LLC
Reedy Press
PO Box 5131
St. Louis, MO 63139, USA
www.reedypress.com

No part of this publication may be reproduced or transmitted in any form or by any means, electronic or mechanical, including photocopy, recording, or any information storage and retrieval system, without permission in writing from the publisher.

Permissions may be sought directly from Reedy Press at the above mailing address or via our website at www.reedypress.com.

Library of Congress Control Number: 2023935797

ISBN: 9781681064611

Design by Jill Halpin

Cover image courtesy of Thomas Keever

Printed in the United States of America
23 24 25 26 27   5 4 3 2 1

We (the publisher and the author) have done our best to provide the most accurate information available when this book was completed. However, we make no warranty, guarantee, or promise about the accuracy, completeness, or currency of the information provided, and we expressly disclaim all warranties, express or implied. Please note that attractions, company names, addresses, websites, and phone numbers are subject to change or closure, and this is outside of our control. We are not responsible for any loss, damage, injury, or inconvenience that may occur due to the use of this book. When exploring new destinations, please do your homework before you go. You are responsible for your own safety and health when using this book.

DEDICATION

Dedicated to the entire crew of Foote Headquarters South—Al, my partner-in-crime, who has been by my side for every adventure, and our daughters Amanda and Erinn.

Rude Awakening, courtesy of Tony Murnahan

CONTENTS

Music and Entertainment

Sports and Recreation

Culture and History

Shopping and Fashion

Apple Crate Naturals, courtesy of Elizabeth Blevins

Halloween at the Bootanical Garden, courtesy of DistiNCtly Fayetteville

PREFACE

Nearly 30 years ago, when my husband was offered a job in Fayetteville, we took a leap of faith and moved from the New York area. We didn't know what to expect. During these early days in town, we jumped in our car each weekend and landed where the day took us. We discovered a fun and friendly area with plenty of activities. Because both long- and short-term residents are from all over the country and the world, we never felt like outsiders.

The love of this area led me to a job with the Fayetteville Area Convention & Visitors Bureau (now DistiNCtly Fayetteville), where I spent more than two decades helping travel writers explore the region. Each visit was catered to the writer's interests, so I got to know the area again, through their eyes. What a gift!

While you may think with two decades in tourism, there may not be much left to discover. Not true! As I researched this book, I discovered new hidden and not-so-hidden gems that I am pleased to share with readers of this book. I hope my *100 Things to Do in Fayetteville Before You Die* serves as a guide to getting to know Fayetteville. As you explore, did you discover something not in the book? Let me know on Twitter at @melodyfooteHQS. I'll add it to my weekend plans.

Anstead's, courtesy of Elizabeth Blevins

ACKNOWLEDGMENTS

Thank you to everyone who introduced me to the community's assets during my career in tourism. Without that nurturing, I may not have discovered many of these treasures. During the development of this book, special recognition is due to the staff at each site who took the time to answer my questions, ensure the accuracy of the listings, and provide photos. Thanks also to Elizabeth Blevins, Tony Murnahan, Casey Ferris, DistiNCtly Fayetteville, and Jason Brady for submitting photos to be considered for inclusion in this book.

Thanks also to my husband, daughters, and friends for tagging along to try new restaurants, explore new sites, and rediscover those we already loved.

Fowler's Barbecue, courtesy of Melody Foote

FOOD AND DRINK

1

SPEND AN AFTERNOON WITH FRIENDS AND FAMILY AT DIRTBAG ALES BREWERY

Dirtbag Ales started when one of its founders, Vernardo "Tito" Simmons-Valenzuela, was serving in the army. He traded a friend a home brew kit for the promise of free beer for life. After many stovetop brews, demand for his product grew, and Dirtbag Ales was born.

Today, the family- and dog-friendly brewery sits just off I-95 in Hope Mills. They boast a taproom with a large selection of brews, a playground, a field for soccer, and a dog park. With plenty of open space and a shady yard, the brewery is a family favorite on Saturday and Sunday afternoons. Bring your chairs, blankets, family, friends, and dogs. Secure a shady spot, grab lunch from a food truck, and spend a lazy afternoon.

5435 Corporation Dr., Hope Mills, 910-426-2537
dirtbagales.com

TIP

Dirtbag's flagship brew, Blood Orange Kolsch, one of Tito's first creations, is always on tap. Another favorite, Mocha Porter, is made with High-Octane Cold Brew Coffee. Be sure to sample both when you visit.

2

STUFF YOURSELF
AT THE FRIED TURKEY SANDWICH SHOP

Visitors from above the Mason-Dixon Line may not know about the wonders of fried turkey, but southerners sure do. Whether fried in oil or air fried, it is a staple of Thanksgiving dinner. And who doesn't enjoy the turkey sandwich leftovers the next day?

When they opened in 2008, the Fried Turkey Sandwich Shop made the turkey sandwich a year-round treat. The restaurant was an instant hit. Today, arrive at noon at one of the Fried Turkey Sandwich shops and expect a line of locals cueing for their chosen comfort food. In addition to hot, sliced turkey that is fried on-site, turkey platters, sandwiches, and salads, the menu offers several specialties such as the Turkey Day Sandwich, which is fried turkey, dressing, and cranberry sauce on Texas toast served with a side of gravy. Thanksgiving dinner, anyone?

1820 Owen Dr., 910-491-7603
2318 Paintersmill Dr., 910-425-2755
friedturkeyshop.com

TIP

Try the Carolina Style Sweet Potato Pie. It is richer than a typical sweet potato pie with a sweet crust.

3

DECIDE ON DECADENCE
AT THE COFFEE SCENE

Each time a Google search directs you to a local coffee house, you can rightfully expect a great cup of coffee. The Coffee Scene is no exception, and it offers so much more. A dazzling case displays a variety of pastries (did someone say cannolis?), and specialty breakfast and lunch sandwiches tease visitors waiting to order their coffee. If that isn't enough, The Coffee Scene serves delicious gelato with flavors like Nutty Buddy, Salted Caramel, and Cotton Candy. Enjoy a drink on the outside patio, lounge on the bottom floor filled with plush couches, or take the winding staircase to the second floor. Special events such as poetry readings and open mic nights happen in the second-floor performance area.

3818 Morganton Rd., 910-864-7948
1504 NC-87, Cameron, 919-343-2195
Womack Army Medical Center, 4-2817 Riley Rd., Fort Liberty
450 Hay St., 910-568-3758
thecoffeesceneinc.com

4

COOL DOWN WITH A NEW ORLEANS–STYLE SNOBALL

AT BIG T'S

Nothing is better on a hot summer day than a sweet cold treat like a Snoball, which is made with fluffy shaved ice and flavoring. That's why Big T's in Hope Mills has a long line at their window on any hot summer day. Big T's serves nearly 75 flavors of Snoballs, including Cake Batter, Egg Custard, Key Lime, Marshmallow, and Minions. They even offer flavors dedicated to local universities and superheroes. If a simple Snoball isn't enough, choose a Snocream, which is sno (fluffy shaved ice) blended with vanilla and flavored cream, or a Frappuccino, which is Sno blended with vanilla ice cream and a Snoball flavor. Both are topped with whipped cream and a cherry. Yum!

Big T's also has a menu with a range of drinks, hamburgers, hot dogs, fries, nachos, and similar items. Its large, covered picnic area overlooks Hope Mills Lake.

3609 N Main St., Hope Mills, 910-568-7722
bigtssnoballs.com

5

WAKE UP
AT RUDE AWAKENING COFFEE HOUSE

Opened in 1999, Rude Awakening Coffee House heralded Fayetteville's downtown renaissance. Owners Bruce and Molly Arnold renovated the condemned circa 1914 building, which once housed Brady's Soda Shop, to its previous splendor.

As committed as the Arnolds were to the renovation of their building, today the commitment extends to serving a great cup of coffee. They serve organic and free-trade brews in your chosen form, alongside a variety of local chocolates and desserts, lunch specials, and other sweet treats. The full menu changes seasonally. Patrons can explore several unique gift items for sale along the walls of the shop. So, grab a coffee and sip it in the lobby, sit at a table along Hay Street and people-watch, or relax in the plant-filled courtyard.

227 Hay St., 910-223-7833 (RUDE)
rudeawakening.net

TIP

During events in downtown Fayetteville, Rude Awakening can get busy, and you may wait for your drink. Plan accordingly.

6

"WINE" DOWN
AT LUIGI'S ITALIAN CHOPHOUSE & BAR

Fayetteville's favorite fine-dining establishment, Luigi's Italian Chophouse & Bar, was founded by Peter Parrous, a Greek immigrant and successful restauranteur, more than 40 years ago.

Still family-run, the upscale restaurant serves Black Angus beef, fresh fish, seafood, and an array of pasta featuring the family's homemade sauces. All sauces and salad dressings are family recipes and are made on-site. While the food is amazing, their wine offerings are the stars of Luigi's show. The extensive wine menu is 48 pages long. Owners started free Thursday-night wine tastings in 1999 and a Wine of the Week program in 2002. Both continue today. In the August 2003 issue of *Wine Spectator Magazine*, Luigi's was awarded an "Award of Excellence" in the magazine's Restaurant Awards Program and has received this recognition every year since.

528 N McPherson Church Rd., 910-864-1810
luigisnc.com

TIP

While not required, make a reservation to secure your time. If you find the wine menu overwhelming, ask your server for a recommendation. They will make a recommendation based on your preferences and your selected dish.

7

TAKE YOUR TASTE BUDS
ON AN AUTHENTIC ADVENTURE AT GRILLED GINGER VIETNAMESE RESTAURANT

Grilled Ginger serves more than 100 Vietnamese dishes, from some of your favorites like pho and vermicelli to others like Shaken Beef, a variety of curries, and Vietnamese calamari. A large variety of vegetarian dishes are on the menu, as are specialty drinks, including Vietnamese coffee, fresh fruit smoothies (Vietnamese style), and whole fresh coconut.

Try the Grilled Ginger Wraps & Roll for a fun adventure. Use all the provided ingredients (rice paper, vegetables, seasonings, vermicelli noodles, a combination of shrimp, chicken, and pork) to create your own rolls. All ingredients are fresh, flavorful, and plentiful. Servings are large, so plan to take some home to save room for dessert. Among dessert options are an Egg Roll Banana Split and Che Trai Cay, which is a fruit dessert with jackfruit, palm tree fruit, longan lychee, and coconut jelly mixed with milk and fruit juice. Delicious!

5052 Yadkin Rd., 910-867-2227
grilledginger.com

TIP

Try all the sauces with your dish or at the table. Each is flavorful and unique.

8

DRINK A NC CRAFT COCKTAIL AT DIRTY WHISKEY COCKTAIL BAR

While Dirty Whiskey is located on the same property as Dirtbag Ales, the vibe couldn't be more different. Dirty Whiskey is not open to anyone under 21, and the upscale interior is perfect for quiet conversations and date nights. They also serve a variety of fresh and unique cocktails not found at Dirtbag Ales.

Updated seasonally by trained Dirty Whiskey mixologists, the specialty cocktail menu features in-house fusions, locally sourced ingredients, and North Carolina spirits. Year-round cocktails include Lavender Bees Knees (gin, lemon juice, honey, lavender, bitters), Whiskey Jam (Mother Earth Whiskey, blueberry jam, lemon juice, simple syrup, rosemary), and The Tiffany (Oak City Amaretto, lemon juice, cherry juice, simple syrup).

Dirty Whiskey strives to offer only NC-produced spirits. In addition to specialty craft cocktails, Dirty Whiskey serves Dirtbag Ales beer. Ashe's Mobile Cigar lounge is connected to Dirty Whiskey via its main patio.

5431 Corporation Dr., Hope Mills, 910-758-7744
dirtywhiskeyinc.com

TIP
Dirty Whiskey serves a fantastic Bloody Mary on Sunday mornings. Enjoy one as you stroll the Dirtbag Ales Farmers Market.

9

EAT BREAKFAST LIKE A LOCAL
AT MILLER'S TOO

Attached to a gas station and a convenience store, Miller's Too is not a traditional hot spot for visitors; however, all the locals know about this hidden gem in western Cumberland County. It's the place to go to grab a quick, inexpensive, and hearty breakfast.

All the southern favorites are on the menu, including homemade grits, hash browns, breakfast burritos, fried bologna, eggs, omelets, massive pancakes, and, of course, bacon, sausage, and breakfast ham. The price is right. A typical breakfast is less than $5 per person.

If breakfast isn't your thing, visit during lunch Monday through Saturday or for dinner on Thursday and Friday. Weekly dinner specials are available alongside menu standards like beef tips, salads, and pork chops.

Miller's Too is open for breakfast and lunch Monday through Saturday and dinner on Thursday and Friday.

7383 Stoney Point Rd., 910-424-9299

10

SET YOUR SWEET TOOTH LOOSE
AT MARCI'S CAKES & BAKES

A stroll down charming Trade Street in Hope Mills is not complete without a visit to Marci's Cakes & Bakes. Stop in, have a coffee, and choose from one of the many sweet treats in the display case. Everything is made on-site and made to perfection.

The store has a down-home feel. Guests are welcome to sit and stay a while or take their treats home. Choose from cupcakes, cookies, macarons, pies, cake pops, and everything in between. Aside from themed weeks around the holidays, the bakery has monthly special weeks such as *Star Wars* and classic video games. Nearly all the treats in the case are tied to the theme. On a recent visit, the Rainbow Road cupcake was an easy favorite, unlike the actual Rainbow Road Mario Kart track.

5474 Trade St., Hope Mills, 910-425-6377
facebook.com/marciscakesandbakes

TIP

The store recently introduced The Oven Mitt Library, which invites patrons to take a book and bring it back or replace it with another.

11

SAVOR SOUTHERN FAVORITES
AT NOBLE MEATS

Located in a nondescript building on a country highway just north of Spring Lake, Noble Meats is easy to miss. So, set your navigation and stay alert because you don't want to miss it.

Visit Monday through Friday, and you'll find the small space packed with patrons eating pulled pork barbecue, pulled chicken, brisket, ribs, burnt ends, rotisserie chicken plates, sandwiches, or tacos. Sides include new potatoes, baked beans, potato salad, red slaw, and Texas Caviar, which is a perfectly seasoned bean and corn casserole. All food is cooked on-site and fresh every day. Noble Meats is also a butcher shop with perfect steaks, ribs, pork chops, and bacon for cooking at home. Much of the Saturday business is at the butcher case.

2469 Lillington Hwy., Spring Lake, 910-436-6022
facebook.com/noblemeats

TIP

Try the Burnt Ends. The pieces are cubed, sauced, and added to the smoker to caramelize. We've heard them called meat candy, for good reason.

DEVOUR YOUR FAVORITE COMFORT FOOD

AT UPTOWN'S CHICKEN AND WAFFLES

Although she was already a local celebrity, when Chef Judy (Judith Cage) won *Supermarket Stakeout* on the Food Network in 2019, she was thrust into the national spotlight. Add a visit to Uptown's Chicken and Waffles to your Fayetteville agenda to experience her unique, award-winning cuisine.

As the name suggests, the hallmark dish at Uptown's Chicken and Waffles is, in fact, chicken and waffles. Diners choose from a chicken breast, wings, or two chicken legs to top their plain, blueberry, or sweet potato waffle for the meal. Pick from house-made sweet honey, bourbon, strawberry, or maple pecan butter for a sweet accompaniment. Seasoned to perfection with a slight kick, the fried chicken is simply flawless and has no comparison. Uptown's offers a full menu in addition to Chicken & Waffles, including Chef Judy's fantastic Shrimp & Grits.

1707 Owen Dr., 910-676-8039
facebook.com/uptownsfay

13

SELECT THE PERFECT SWEET
AT FROSTINGS CAKESHOP

Do you have a family that can't agree, even when you are offering a special treat? Make plans to visit Frostings Cakeshop.

Frostings was founded by Palaran and Solomon Miller when they decided to turn Palaran's love of baking into a business. She is the head baker and decides the flavors that are offered daily. With each location offering up to 25 types of cupcakes each day, the pickiest people in your party is bound to find a flavor that is perfect for their palate. A sample menu may include Strawberry Lemonade, Wedding Cake, Cotton Candy, Boston Crème, Birthday Cake, Triple Salted Caramel, Oreo Truffle, Red Velvet, and Pineapple Upside Down Cake.

Frostings also offers macaroons, cakes, coffee, and cookies.

3550 Footbridge Ln., Hope Mills, 910-987-9628
1538 NC-87, Cameron, 910-987-9356
facebook.com/frostingscakeshop

TIP

If available when you visit, try the Ube (purple yam) flavored cake. Ube is a flavor unique to the Philippines, where Palaran was raised.

14

SAMPLE ALL THE SOUTHERN FAVORITES
AT GRANDSONS RESTAURANT

Located just off of I-95 Exit 40, Grandsons restaurant, a large southern buffet, is a favorite of both locals and I-95 travelers. Wondering about the name? Fred Chason opened his restaurant in 1980 and closed in 1997. His grandson opened Grandsons in Hope Mills in 2005, using many of his grandfather's recipes. It was an instant hit.

The restaurant serves a variety of southern favorites, including barbecue, fried chicken, chicken and dumplings, fish, yams, ribs, salad, and lots of veggies and beans cooked in classic southern style. Don't sample too much so you can save room for one of the cobblers, pies, or ice cream for dessert. Patrons enjoy their meal in the large casual restaurant decorated as a large picnic area. Drink refills are free and plentiful.

5339 Marracco Dr., Hope Mills, 910-860-4899
facebook.com/grandsonshopemills

TIP

If you hate waiting in line, arrive a little bit early or after the standard lunch and dinner hours, especially on the weekends.

15

GRAB GREEK FAVORITES
AT ZORBA'S GYRO

Ask anyone in Fayetteville where to get a great gyro, and you'll probably hear something like "Zorba's, duh." Three different types of filling gyros and souvlaki are available on fresh pitas daily. Diners looking for something lighter can try chicken and veggie pitas. The price is right—a filling gyro and a drink are less than $10.

A variety of other Greek and American specialties round out the lunch and dinner menu. Consider baked feta, tzatziki with pita wedges, or spanakopita as appetizers while you wait for your meal. You won't be sorry.

Leaving Zorba's hungry is never an issue. However, consider saving room for or taking home one of Marina's brownies for dessert.

The family-run business now operates in two locations.

2919 Raeford Rd., 910-484-1010
3114 N Main St., Hope Mills, 910-424-3332
zorbasgyro.com

Stop by Zorba's in the morning for an inexpensive and filling breakfast. The Zorba's special two farm fresh eggs (any style), a choice of grits or hash brown potatoes, and a choice of two buttermilk pancakes or toast and jelly is less than $6.

PURSUE SANDWICH PERFECTION
AT PAN

While it's a safe bet to say you've had plenty of sandwiches in your lifetime, you've never had a sandwich like Pan's sandwiches. The breakfast and lunch restaurant uses many locally sourced meats, fresh-baked bread, cheeses, and produce to create sandwiches and salads with unique and fresh flavors. All toppings, dressings, and condiments, including the favorite lemon pistachio vinaigrette, are made in-house.

Offerings include the vegetarian Stace (balsamic vinaigrette, fresh mozzarella, roasted red peppers, roasted artichokes, basil pesto), the Waiting on a Train (mortadella, milano salami, provolone, roasted red peppers, lemon pistachio vinaigrette), and the Lafayette panini (mortadella, goat cheese, artichokes, red pesto, Dijon aioli).

While you could choose Carolina Kettle chips as a sandwich side, consider the pesto and cheese tortellini or the basaltic cucumber salad. You won't be sorry.

Pan also has a morning menu with breakfast sandwiches, local coffees, and fresh muffins.

105 Hay St., 910-491-3105
facebook.com/panfaync

DIP INTO GREEK LIFE
AT FAYETTEVILLE'S GREEK FESTIVAL

Each year in mid-September, Fayetteville Greek Festival takes patrons on a tour of Greece. While the Greek music, dance, and vendors selling Greek goods are fun and worthy of a visit, the food and drink are the stars of the show. The festival is held at Saints Constantine and Helen Greek Orthodox Church.

Visit the festival for lunch or dinner during a typical year and choose from a variety of salads and gyros, souvlaki, dolmades, and *pastichio*, a favorite described as a Greek lasagna-like dish. Save room for 10 types of Greek pastries, all of which are handmade by members of the church and baked on-site. The adventure your taste buds are on doesn't end with the drinks. Choose from a variety of Greek and American beer and wine; Ouzo, a traditional Greek spirit; and soft drinks.

So, pick your pleasure, grab a seat, and relax while you enjoy the music, dancing, and a taste of Greece.

614 Oakridge Ave., 910-484-2010
faygreekchurch.com/greekfestival

TIP

If you miss the Greek festival, you'll have another opportunity to grab some Greek pastries. "The World's Largest Spaghetti Dinner," held each November, features spaghetti and pastries.

SMOKE, DRINK, AND BE SOCIAL

AT ANSTEAD'S CIGAR BAR AND LOUNGE

Originally located in the local mall, Anstead's Tobacco Company has offered cigars and tobacco products since 1975. In 2013, they moved to a new location, greatly expanded the selection of cigars and pipe products, and opened the 2,500-square-foot upscale Craft Cigar Bar and Lounge. The humidor selection includes Davidoff, Arturo Fuente, Liga Privada, Opus X, Montecristo, and many more.

Decorated with tables, large plush chairs, couches, and large-screen TVs, the two-floor lounge is the perfect location to watch a game with a group or have an intimate conversation.

The Craft Cigar Bar's unique craft cocktail menu is updated seasonally, but the classic Old Fashioned or the lesser-known Last Word always makes the list. Bourbons typically available include Woodford, Old Forester, Uncle Nearest, and Booker's. A signature scotch offering is a Macallan Flight, featuring the rare Macallan 25 Year.

320 N McPherson Church Rd., 910-864-5705
ansteads.com

TIP
Watch the calendar for Anstead's special events. Cigar manufacturers from around the country routinely visit the lounge.

DELIGHT IN LOCAL FLAVORS
AT NAPKINS SUNDAY BRUNCH

Each Sunday morning, the chef at Napkins shops at the Dirtbag Ales Farmers Market for inspiration. At about 12:30, the restaurant opens with a special brunch menu featuring the market-inspired dish (or dishes) alongside their regular menu.

The menu changes seasonally and showcases the creativity of the restaurant staff with changing menu features. The restaurant, located on the grounds of Dirtbag Ales, was well known and loved for its burgers, hand-cut French fries, and fried Brussels sprouts with its own dipping sauce. In late 2022, they tweaked their menu to offer even more locally sourced dishes, and the public responded enthusiastically. Favorite seasonal items include doner kebab, poke bowls, and grilled chicken wraps. Their famous fried Brussels sprouts with handmade dipping sauce remains on the menu year-round.

5435 Corporation Dr., Ste. 2, Hope Mills, 910-489-4857
graybillhospitality.com

TIP

Don't miss Oktoberfest at Dirtbag Ales. Napkins serves a delicious German-inspired Oktoberfest menu.

SIP A TEA COCKTAIL
AT WINTERBLOOM TEA

Don't worry if you walk into Winterbloom Tea unsure of what you'd like to try because the staff has you covered. Explain what you like or how you are feeling, and they can recommend and create a customized drink. Each brew is timed, so your tea is steeped to perfection. Enjoy yours hot or cold.

Shortly after opening in 2016, Fayetteville's only tea shop quickly became a local favorite and a must-visit location in downtown Fayetteville.

After extensive research, the owner Josh Choi expanded the store's offerings and created exclusive and unique tea-infused cocktails. Favorites include locally themed "Lafayette," made with cardamom and rosebud tea, lemon, orange, and rose vodka, and "Hemingway," made with jasmine green tea and peppermint mixed with absinthe, grapefruit, rose, and elderflower.

238 Hay St., 910-491-3536
facebook.com/winterbloomtea

21

TANTALIZE YOUR TASTE BUDS

AT FOWLER'S BARBECUE

Veteran-owned Fowler's Barbecue redefines southern barbecue. This scratch-made kitchen uses many fresh North Carolina ingredients in its food, and the food is stellar. (Just check the reviews!) Most items on their menu are made on-site, including sauces, pickles, pimento cheese, croutons, salad, and slaw dressings.

Fowler's is open Wednesday through Saturday for lunch, and the choices are plentiful. The brisket, barbecue, chicken, and ribs are seasoned to perfection. Either a meat plate with two sides or a specialty sandwich are solid lunch choices. Favorite sandwiches include "The Angry Hawaiian" (pulled pork or pulled chicken with jalapenos, pineapple, and a spicy teriyaki sauce) and "The Commander 'n Cheese" (brisket served with pimento cheese, house pickles, and a sweet barbecue sauce).

Consider the smoked potato salad as your side; you've never tasted anything like it. Another solid choice is baked beans or fresh-cut fries. Whatever you decide to eat, beat the crowds, and arrive early. When the day's food is gone, it's gone.

723 W Rowan St., 910-491-5721
facebook.com/fowlersbarbecue

TIP

If you arrive on the day burnt ends are served, add them to your order. You're welcome.

Cameo Theatre, courtesy of Elizabeth Blevins

MUSIC AND ENTERTAINMENT

22

APPRECIATE MUSICAL EXCELLENCE
WITH THE FAYETTEVILLE SYMPHONY ORCHESTRA

Founded in 1956, the Fayetteville Symphony Orchestra is a professional regional orchestra whose mission is to educate, entertain, and inspire its audiences. A season of eight concerts, each with a specific theme, are staged each year. Season performance themes may include "Holiday Brass," "The Music of John Williams," and "Songs of Love." Full-season and individual tickets are sold for the shows, which are staged at Methodist University, Fayetteville State University, and local churches.

Additionally, there are plenty of opportunities to engage with the symphony for free. Three to four Community Concerts are offered each year. A new series titled "Symphony on Tap," showcases symphony musicians at local breweries. The Symphony on Tap performances feature small groups of symphony musicians such as the Jazz Quartet, String Quartet, and various duets.

310 Green St., 910-433-4690
fayettevillesymphony.org

ENJOY THE SOUNDS OF SUMMER

AT FAYETTEVILLE AFTER FIVE

Head to Festival Park in downtown Fayetteville on the second Friday in the summer months to enjoy a free summer concert, courtesy of the Fayetteville Dogwood Festival. The gates open at 5 p.m., and the opening act starts at 6 p.m. followed by a headliner. Concerts feature different types of music, so check the website to find your favorite.

Although coolers and outside food are not allowed in the park, five to seven food trucks are available on-site. You also can spend a leisurely evening in downtown Fayetteville and grab dinner at one of the region's eateries. So, open your lawn chairs or spread out your blanket, and enjoy the free summer show. Plan your visit on the right night, and you can enjoy some music while you eat dinner from a local food truck, and then walk down the street to catch a Woodpecker's game.

335 Ray Ave., 910-323-1934
thedogwoodfestival.com

24

REJOICE IN THE SEASON
AT THE SINGING CHRISTMAS TREE

A Fayetteville tradition for more than 40 years, Snyder Memorial Baptist Church stages a massive Singing Christmas Tree show in the week just after Thanksgiving. Each year, the church builds a 30-foot tall tree in the center of its sanctuary. A large choir fills the tree's branches, appearing like ornaments on the tree. The church has a large music ministry, which adds a variety of choirs, musical ensembles, and stellar solo artists to the program. The full orchestra, kids choirs and handbell choirs, and state-of-the-art technical elements are highlights.

There is no cost to attend the Singing Christmas tree. However, because of its popularity, you must secure tickets for the show. They are available in mid-November from the Church office.

701 Westmont Dr., 910-484-3191
snydermbc.com

25

ESCAPE MOVIE MEGAPLEXES AT CAMEO ART HOUSE THEATRE

Patrons at Cameo Art House Theatre typically do not watch the latest blockbusters that populate larger theater complexes. The Cameo showcases art, independent, foreign, and classic films. Its building was once home to one of Fayetteville's first motion picture theaters, the New Dixie. Owners purchased the building in the late 1990s and renovated the building to its 1920s splendor before opening in 2000. The main theater has 125 velvet-covered cast-iron opera-style chairs, and the upstairs Loge theater has 38 stadium-style super comfortable seats that offer an intimate screening. Preservation North Carolina recognized the mixed-use rehabilitation of the Cameo. The theater was also recognized for its commitment to highlighting independent films in the Sundance Film Festival program.

225 Hay St., 910-486-6633
cameoarthouse.com

TIP

Arrive early and grab a glass of wine, beer, or cappuccino, and enjoy it with friends or your date before the show.

LOVE LOCAL THEATER
AT THE CAPE FEAR REGIONAL THEATRE

Founded in 1962 as a community theater named The Fayetteville Little Theatre, the Cape Fear Regional Theatre (CFRT) is an award-winning professional theater that is said to be one of the finest in the state. The theater, which features a three-story complex with a 300-seat main stage, contracts actors, writers, and designers from throughout the country. Each year, CFRT's six-show season along with their various educational programs reach 49,000 audience members. This includes nearly 22,000 K–12 students from schools around the Fayetteville region. The theater also rents their facility for special public events. It continues the more than three decade-long tradition of hosting "The Greatest Christmas Pageant Ever" each December. The show features local children and adult actors in up to four distinct groups of performers, each with their own days and nights on the stage.

1209 Hay St., 910-323-4233
cfrt.org

TIP

CFRT is unique in that it won awards first as a community theater and later as a professional theater.

SING HALLELUJAH
AT MESSIAH SING

Each December, as a gift to the community, Cumberland Choral Arts and the Fayetteville Symphony partner to offer a free performance of Handel's *Messiah.* The annual concerts rotate among churches in the region. Aside from the beautiful music, this concert is special because audience members are invited to bring their scores and sing along with the choir and orchestra. This tradition began during the early days of Cumberland Choral Arts' 30-year history.

Soloists receive key roles for the performance. Past soloists have included members of Cumberland Choral Arts, singers from the Fayetteville area, and singers from other parts of North Carolina.

In addition to the Messiah Sing concert, the company performs at least four concerts a year, where they sing classical works as well as favorites from screen, jazz, and opera.

109 Hay St., Ste. 202, 910-303-0463
cumberlandchoralarts.org

28

STEP INTO A WINTER WONDERLAND

AT HOLIDAY LIGHTS AT THE GARDEN

Each weekend in December and daily just before the holidays, Cape Fear Botanical Garden lights up its gardens and walkways with more than 1 million lights for its annual "Holiday Lights at the Garden" event. Santa and the Grinch attend, and a variety of activities are offered along the walking trails that meander through the stunning lights. Food trucks are on-site, and entertainment is provided each evening.

While at the event, shop for unique gifts at the Holiday Vendor Market, where local artisans and crafters sell and showcase their products. The Garden Gift Shop is also open for the perfect garden find. Tickets are required and must be purchased in advance. Follow the Garden's Facebook page for an update on each evening's food trucks and entertainment.

536 N Eastern Blvd., 910-486-0221
capefearbg.org

EMBRACE YOUR INNER IRISH

AT PADDY'S IRISH PUB

Owner Patrick "Paddy" Gibney came to Fayetteville from Dublin, Ireland, in 1987 as a high school exchange student. Twenty years later, he opened Fayetteville's first Irish Pub. In 2016, Paddy's was completely renovated and expanded to include a state-of-the-art lounge and event center called The Church. The bar serves not only perfectly poured Guinness and other brews but also specialty crafted cocktails, mixed drinks, and wine. By far, the beverages are not the only reason to visit Paddy's. Live music, trivia, "kilted" karaoke, and "Comedy & Cocktails" round out weekly entertainment. Enjoy a drink on the spacious patio on a nice evening for an instant mini-vacation. The pub and patio's decor showcases both Irish heritage and the local community, and it's wrapped in a bawdy sense of humor.

2606 Raeford Rd., Ste. B, 910-568-5654
paddysirishpub.com

TIP

Check out the wall with photos of the famous people Paddy has met.

30

GET LIT
WITH SWEET TEA SHAKESPEARE

Fayetteville's classic theater and music company, Sweet Tea Shakespeare (STS), performs Shakespeare and other classics at venues throughout Fayetteville and Raleigh. In the Shakespearean tradition, audiences surround the central performance space, which has simple staging. Prior to the show, audiences enjoy live music, often with audience engagement and tasty local eats. In addition to classic Shakespeare, the company is known for a couple of nontraditional shows. This isn't stuffy Shakespeare; STS presents classic stories with a contemporary vibe.

Want to experience Shakespeare in a different way? Attend Lit, Sweet Tea Shakespeare's irreverent celebration of Shakespeare. The Lit shows are held at restaurants, breweries, and arts venues. Filled with music, improv, drinking games, and audience interaction, the Lit series is a laughter-filled event.

Each holiday season, Sweet Tea's Behold: A Christmas Folk Cantata rings in the season. The lineup for Behold changes each year, but it always features traditional and original live music and thought-provoking reflections.

126 Hay St., 910-420-4383
sweetteashakespeare.com

SIP, PAINT, AND LAUGH
AT WINE, PAINT & CREATE

Looking for a different idea for ladies' night or date night? Book a party at Wine, Paint & Create in Hope Mills. Pick up wine, beer, and snacks, and show up for an evening of fun creativity. Corkscrews and glasses are on-site. Arrive a little before the booked party time to open wine and chat with your painting partners.

All supplies are set up prior to party time. The Wine, Paint & Create team provides the paint, brushes, canvas, easel, and an artist who will paint the night's selection with the partygoers. Attendees are guided step-by-step to create their own version of the evening's 16 x 20 masterpiece. To register, search the calendar for your painting of choice, and register for that class. Then, show up and have fun!

3350 Footbridge Ln., Hope Mills, 910-308-9544
WinePaintCreate.com

32

CELEBRATE SPRING
AT THE FAYETTEVILLE DOGWOOD FESTIVAL

One of Fayetteville's hallmark events, the Fayetteville Dogwood Festival, welcomes nearly 200,000 people to downtown Fayetteville each year over the last weekend in April. For more than four decades, the festival has been the community's unofficial welcome to spring.

On Friday, the festival opens with live entertainment from a nationally recognized act on stage at Festival Park. Nearby, indulge your sweet (or savory) tooth, and chow down on fair foods from local vendors. A full carnival with games and rides also provides entertainment for the entire family.

On Saturday, the festival adds a massive downtown street fair with vendors that include arts and crafts and commercial products. The youngest attendees will love the Kids Zone, where they can create and learn. The fun continues Sunday afternoon and concludes that evening. Local, regional, and national musical acts perform throughout the special event.

335 Ray Ave., 910-323-1934
thedogwoodfestival.com

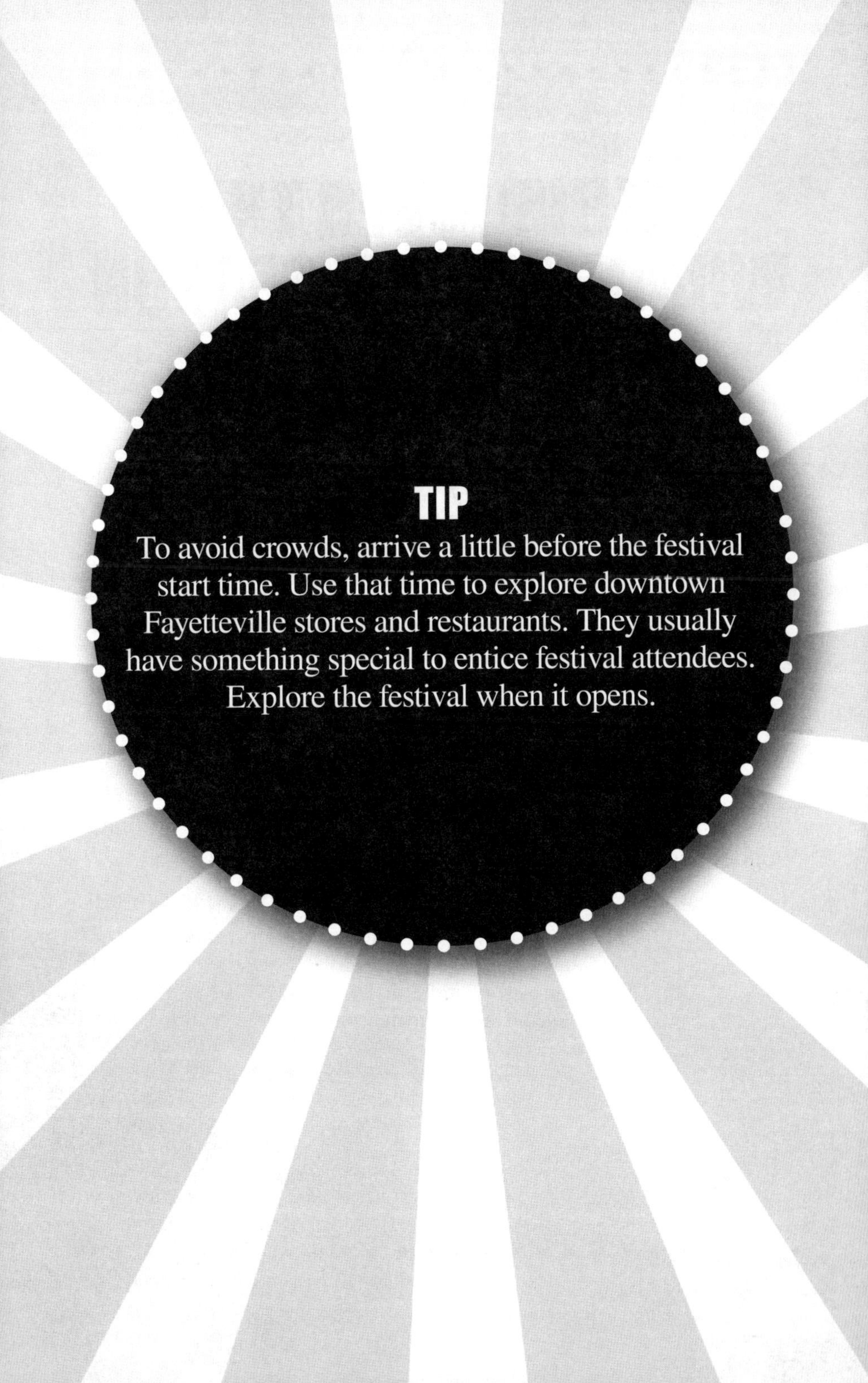
TIP
To avoid crowds, arrive a little before the festival start time. Use that time to explore downtown Fayetteville stores and restaurants. They usually have something special to entice festival attendees. Explore the festival when it opens.

33

REDISCOVER THE WONDER OF THE SEASON

AT SWEET VALLEY RANCH FESTIVAL OF LIGHTS

Each December, Sweet Valley Ranch transforms its 300-acre working ranch into a magical site for the Festival of Lights. To get ready, staff strings more than 1 million lights throughout the farm. Most of the 350 animals that live at Sweet Valley Ranch are on display, and some are part of the show. Visitors drive through the farm to marvel at the lights and exhibits, which are updated each year. Past favorites are a nativity scene with a donkey and camel nearby, a *Star Wars*–themed section, and a military tribute.

After driving through the meandering route and admiring the lights, consider taking some extra time and exploring Tiny's Winter Wonderland across the street. At Tiny's Winter Wonderland, you can visit Santa, shop from a variety of vendors, explore a gift shop, and indulge in some hot chocolate and other treats.

2990 Sunnyside School Rd., 844-622-3276
sweetvalleyranchnc.com

34

HONOR THE LEGACY OF LOCAL AGRICULTURE
AT THE CUMBERLAND COUNTY FAIR

Each year in early September, the grounds of the Crown Complex host the Cumberland County Fair. It's the perfect place to see a variety of products that were submitted to compete for a first, second, or third place ribbon. Entries are in youth and adult categories and include clothing, arts & crafts, jams & jellies, 4-H displays, agriculture, and horticulture. Venture into the livestock area, and explore the youth livestock show and sale. Typically, goats, sheep, horses, cattle, hogs, and chickens are on display. Outside of the agricultural displays, a full carnival fills the large parking lot with rides, games, vendors, and food. Local and regional acts perform throughout the fair's run on an outside stage.

Special admission promotions are offered each day, so check the website to plan your visit.

1960 Coliseum Dr., 910-438-4100
cumberlandcountyfair.org

35

PAINT YOUR MASTERPIECE
AT GREG'S ART, POTTERY & GIFTS

Let your creative side loose and create a one-of-a-kind painted piece of pottery at Greg's Art, Pottery & Gifts. The store has plenty of unpainted pottery to choose from—three walls full, in fact. Simply select your piece, choose colors, and then spend an hour (or a few hours) designing the final product. All supplies are provided by friendly, helpful staff, and the activity is perfect for kids to adults. There is more to Greg's than painting pottery. Named for local artist and potter Greg Hathaway (and owned by his daughter), the store sells his handmade creations as well as other unique gift items. No appointments are necessary to paint, but they are recommended for large groups and on rainy afternoons.

122 Maxwell St., 910-483-8355
facebook.com/gregspottery

STEP BACK IN TIME
AT A DICKENS HOLIDAY

For more than two decades, A Dickens Holiday has brought the magic and wonder of a Victorian Christmas to downtown Fayetteville. Staged by Fayetteville's Downtown Alliance, Dickens festivities are centered around downtown's historic Victorian-era train station, which is also the Fayetteville History Museum, located at the intersection of Franklin and Maxwell Streets. Dickens's most well-known characters wander the corridor, interacting with visitors and each other. Do not miss Scrooge, who loves to "harass" shoppers, and Marley, as they walk through the festival. Horse-drawn carriages trot slowly along Franklin Street while attendees, many wearing their Victorian-era best, shop the unique stores and vendors lining the streets. Choirs and bands offer traditional holiday music and dancers perform throughout the day. As the sun sets, candles are distributed for a holiday illumination on the museum lawn.

222 Hay St.
faydta.com

TIP

Nearby, the Fayetteville/Cumberland County Arts Council holds Holidays on Hay. The festivals are connected by food trucks. Make time to visit both.

37

TRAVEL THE GALAXY
AT FAYETTEVILLE STATE PLANETARIUM

Be sure to add a visit to the Fayetteville State Planetarium to your Fayetteville to-do list. After renovations, the planetarium reopened in mid-2022 with the highest on-dome resolution of any planetarium in the world. Ten 4K projectors project the night sky as it appears from anywhere on Earth on the facility's 30-foot dome. Attendees can view any part of our galaxy, thousands of other galaxies, and all 88 constellations. They can even see the night sky of the past and the future. A 6,500-watt sound system complements the visual presentation in the 65-seat theater. Themed public shows are held every other Saturday night with an astronomer. Purchase tickets in advance on the Fayetteville State University website. After the show, presenters may offer the opportunity to view the night sky through powerful telescopes. If you get this opportunity, take it.

1200 Murchison Rd., 910-672-1759
uncfsu.edu/community/planetarium

TIP

The planetarium is located in the Lyons Science Building. Go through the main entrance to the campus. The Lyons Science building is the last building on the left before crossing the railroad tracks. Signs will direct you to the planetarium.

SAVOR LOCAL THEATER
AT THE GILBERT THEATER

Gilbert Theater is a semiprofessional, community-minded theater that was founded in 1994 in the basement of the founding artistic director. The black box basement theater had 40 seats and patrons were seated by order of height so everyone could all see the show. The original performances were free. The Gilbert proved so popular that the company moved to a permanent spot in downtown Fayetteville a few years later.

Although the current location is still small and intimate, with seating for about 100, the Gilbert Theater has a diverse following and a reputation for innovation. The company tackles complex and controversial subjects and often showcases up-and-coming playwrights.

Five to six shows are staged each year. Showtimes are typically Friday through Sunday, and tickets are available on the website or 30 minutes prior to showtime on-site.

116 Green St., 910-678-7186
gilberttheater.org

ZipQuest, courtesy of DistiNCtly Fayetteville

SPORTS AND RECREATION

GET NOSTALGIC
AT STOP BUTTON BAR

Look no further than Stop Button Bar for a unique entertainment experience.

Classic arcade games such as Ms. Pacman, Frogger, and Guitar Hero, along with pinball machines and racing simulators, line the walls at Stop Button, and they are all free to play. That's right! For a small admission fee, all games at Stop Button are free to play. Additionally, in the bar area, guests can reserve games from popular game systems, such as PlayStation, Xbox, and Nintendo Switch, and play on-site. Stop Button hosts a variety of tournaments and karaoke throughout the month. Check their Facebook or Instagram pages for dates.

The bar's beverage menu features a nerd-themed cocktail menu and a wide variety of domestic and NC craft beers alongside nonalcoholic drinks.

Open daily, Stop Button Bar is open to guests under 18 throughout the week. After 9 p.m. on Friday and Saturday, admission is limited to anyone over 18 years old.

4251 Legion Rd., Hope Mills, 910-491-1082
stopbuttonbar.com

PLAY A GAME
AT PUTT-PUTT GOLF & GAMES

Putt-Putt Golf started in 1954 when Don Clayton built the first course in Fayetteville. The games were just 25 cents each, and the course was packed. He opened several courses around the community. A few years after opening the Fayetteville-based courses, the company soon began franchising its branded miniature golf game, and Putt-Putt spread across the country. Courses were built to exact specifications to ensure a consistent skill-based experience at any Putt-Putt location.

Today, Cumberland County is home to one franchise, Putt-Putt Golf & Games at the Millstone Complex. It's the perfect place for an afternoon of family fun or an outing for two. Visitors can choose from two 18-hole Putt-Putt Golf courses, a large arcade, a go-kart track, bumper boats, and a two-story laser tag arena. Putt-Putt has weekly and daily multi-attraction specials.

3311 Footbridge Ln., Hope Mills, 910-424-7888
puttputt.com

RELEASE YOUR INNER ADVENTURER
AT ZIPQUEST WATERFALL & TREETOP ADVENTURE

After climbing to the first platform to start a ZipQuest Waterfall Expedition, your feet won't touch the ground for 2-½ hours. Ranked by *USA Today* as one of the Top 10 zip lines in the United States, a ZipQuest experience includes up to eight tree-to-tree zip lines that go to a two-story waterfall and climb as high as 80 feet, three canopy sky bridges over 100 feet long each, three spiral staircases, and 16 unique tree platforms.

Guests' safety is a top concern at ZipQuest. Everyone, including two trained guides on each tour, is always connected to the tree or the course. Guides are trained for safety and fun, and they are also experts in the ecology of the park. Three courses are available—a Waterfall Expedition, a shorter Treetop Excursion, and NightQuest, a tour with headlamps.

533 Carvers Falls Rd., 910-488-8787
zipquest.com

TIP

Each tree has a name. Ask the guides while on your tour.

42

SOAR
AT PARACLETEXP

Bet you didn't know you can fly. Well, you can at ParacleteXP, the largest indoor skydiving wind tunnel in the United States. A Paraclete experience is not a ride or a simulator, but a flight in an indoor wind tunnel, which simulates a free fall during a parachute jump. But don't worry, you don't have to go it alone. Classes train you and provide all the fundamentals and equipment needed for the flight. After the 45-minute training session, you strap on all the needed gear and take your guided flight. An instructor joins you in the tunnel for your flight.

Not the adventurous sort? It's free to watch the flyers in the tunnel. Arrive on the right day and you might see a world-famous US Army team training.

190 Paraclete Dr., 910-848-2600
paracletexp.com

43

GET UP CLOSE WITH NATURE
AT CLARK PARK AND NATURE CENTER

The long road to Clark Park and Nature Center is a great transition from a busy area of Fayetteville to a beautiful and quiet corner of the community. In addition to three easy walking trails with plenty of scenic areas, playgrounds, and a campground, the woodland oasis is home to an indoor Nature Center, Kids in Parks Track Trail, and a StoryWalk.

The Kids in Parks Track Trail at Clark Park is one in a network of trails across the country. Activities along the .3-mile trail are designed to turn a visit into an adventure. Kids can even register their completed activities at kidsinparks.com to earn prizes.

Nearby, kids of all ages will wonder at the exhibits and live animals at the Clark Park Nature Center. Turtles, snakes, lizards, and even an alligator are on display. Static presentations on a number of nature science projects include trail camera footage showing the critters that live in the park. After your visit, consider picnicking on the back deck overlooking the woods and waterfall.

631 Sherman Dr., 910-433-1579
fcpr.us

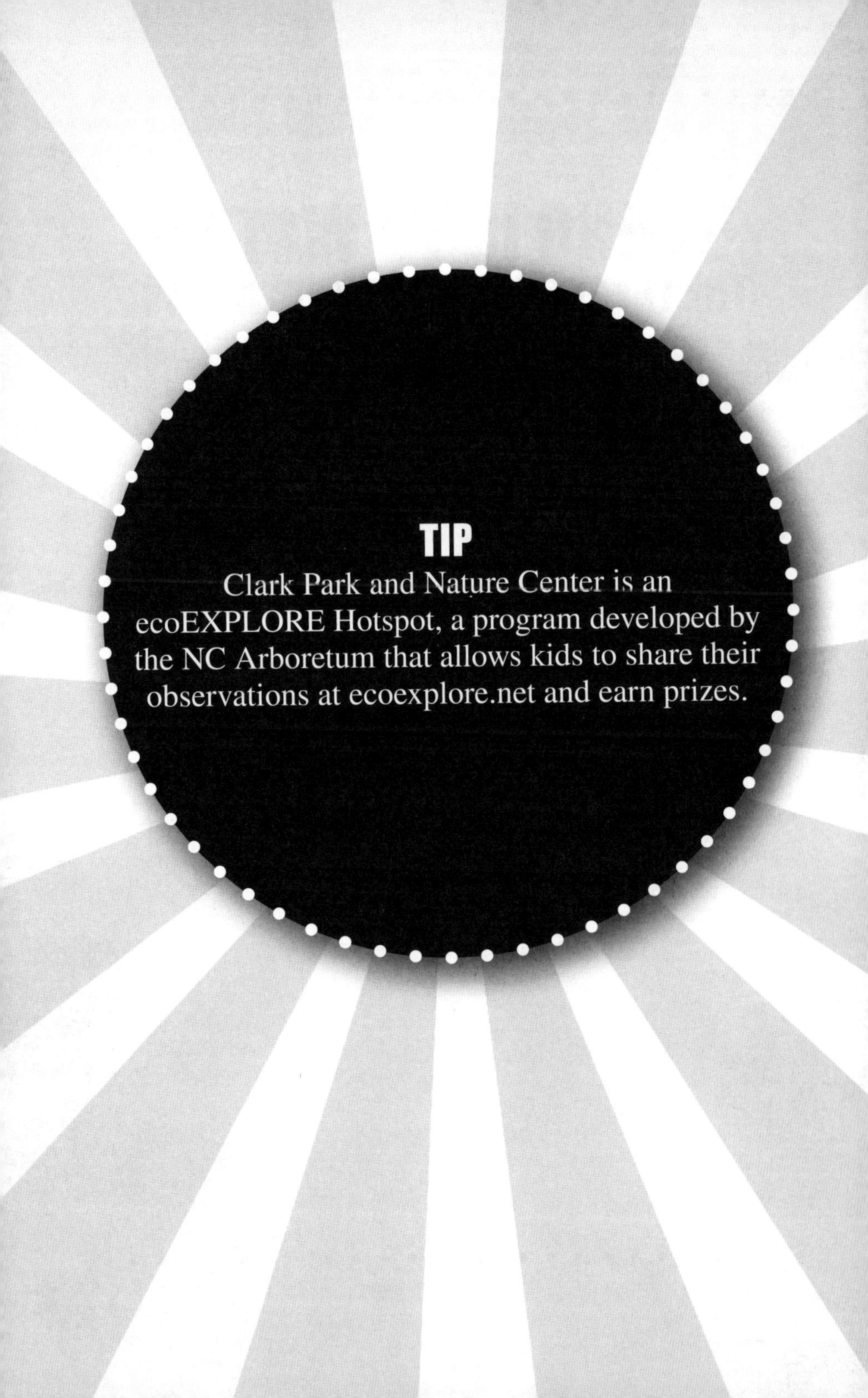

TIP
Clark Park and Nature Center is an ecoEXPLORE Hotspot, a program developed by the NC Arboretum that allows kids to share their observations at ecoexplore.net and earn prizes.

SWING IN TO WATCH
THE FAYETTEVILLE WOODPECKERS

When the Astros selected Fayetteville as the location for the Woodpeckers, they ensured the stadium had the amenities of a larger city's stadium. They hit the mark. Shortly after opening in 2019, the ballpark was named "Ballpark of the Decade" by *Ballpark Magazine*.

During every game, Healy's bar on the third baseline is packed with fans with a front-row seat to all the Woodpeckers' action. Couches, chairs, bar tables, and cornhole games surround the bar area. Throughout the stadium, local and North Carolina beers are featured options. Patrons choose from a variety of seating options. Table service? Rocking chairs? Yes, please.

Food can be classified as standard ballpark fare with a southern flare. Many of the concession stands pay tribute to the community's military heritage. It all comes together to make a perfect baseball experience.

460 Hay St., 910-339-1989
milb.com/fayetteville

LEARN TO FISH
AT JOHN E. PECHMANN FISHING EDUCATION CENTER

The only fishing education center of its kind in North Carolina, the John E. Pechmann Fishing Education Center provides free fishing and aquatic education programs for all ages and abilities throughout the year. The center offers stocked fishing ponds that are open to the public during special events.

The Wildlife Expo, held in the early fall, includes hands-on, interactive exhibits and demonstrations to learn about the natural environment and the roles hunting and fishing play in North Carolina's fish and wildlife conservation. Register for the Expo to spend a few hours fishing the Center's ponds. Tackle and bait are provided for free, and staff is on hand to assist. Bring snacks and arrive early to secure your spot. Visitors travel for several hours to enjoy this unique fishing experience.

7489 Raeford Rd., 910-868-5003
ncwildlife.org

TIP

If you have children that you would like to encourage to fish, attend the annual Family Fishing Day. All equipment is provided, and most kids catch something from the stocked ponds.

46

GET LOST
AT GALLBERRY CORN MAZE

In North Carolina, visiting a corn maze is as fall as pumpkins, colorful mums, and the changing leaves. Gallberry Corn Maze in Hope Mills is a local favorite.

The corn maze isn't actually made from corn; it's made from tall stalks of sorghum, but you won't know the difference. You'll explore six acres of trails that create a marvelous design and an intricate puzzle. Each year's design features some aspect of farm life. A "Maze Cop" is always on the top of a tall observation tower watching for lost explorers. Bring a flashlight and explore after dark for a spookier experience.

Gallberry is more than a corn maze. Admission includes nearly 20 attractions and a Fairy Tale Maze for the younger visitors.

5991 Braxton Rd., Hope Mills, 910-309-7582
gallberrycornmaze.com

ROOT
FOR THE FAYETTEVILLE MARKSMEN

From October through April, fans get their live hockey fix right here in Fayetteville. Several times a month, the Fayetteville Marksmen, a member of the Southern Professional Hockey League, take on opponents at the Crown Coliseum.

While each game is filled with fun, fast hockey action, each game night is different. Every home game is themed, such as Elvis Night, Star Wars, and Pucks and Paws night. Yes, dogs attend that game in a special section of seats. So, if you love hockey and dogs, this special night is for you!

Every Sunday home game is a "Salute to Service" game that honors active service persons and veterans of the Sandhills. At every game, the Marksmen also host and spotlight a local nonprofit to help share their story and make a difference in the Fayetteville area.

1960 Coliseum Dr., 910-321-0123
marksmenhockey.com

48

UNWIND
AT THE CAVE HALOTHERAPY AND SPA

Halotherapy, better known as salt therapy, is said to offer many benefits, including improving circulation, maintaining healthy blood pressure, aiding in hydration, and boosting immunity. The Cape Halotherapy and Spa provides a range of salt treatments, including 45-minute sessions in the only Salt Cave in the region. Sitting in the Salt Cave can be compared to relaxing on the beach in the salty air. Currently, five visitors can visit the Cave each session. No electronics or outside food are allowed. One option is a charcuterie tray and bottomless mimosas for your visit.

In addition to salt therapies, patrons can choose from traditional spa offerings such as massages, facials, detox therapies, and various soaks for individuals and couples.

3320 N Main St., Hope Mills, 910-491-2575
facebook.com/thecavespanc

DRAG YOURSELF TO DOWNTOWN FAYETTEVILLE

FOR THE ZOMBIE WALK AND PROM

Each year, just before Halloween, the undead roam the streets of downtown Fayetteville during the area's favorite family-friendly zombie event. Visitors and residents don their best zombie makeup and attire and roam downtown during a special Fourth Friday. Makeup artists are on hand to bring out each attendee's undead look. At a specified time, zombies gather in one location before parading together down Hay Street, downtown's main thoroughfare. Spectators watch on 20-foot sidewalks and cheer the undead as they meander along the route.

The Zombie walk, hosted by the Cool Spring Downtown District, is scheduled annually during October's Fourth Friday. Fourth Friday is a free monthly event that showcases artists, performers, vendors, and the merchant community in downtown Fayetteville. Before and after the zombie walk, downtown Fayetteville will offer plenty to keep the family entertained.

222 Hay St., 910-223-1089
visitdowntownfayetteville.com

STEP INTO NATURE
AT THE CAPE FEAR BOTANICAL GARDEN

Located on nearly 80 acres just two miles from downtown Fayetteville, the Cape Fear Botanical Garden is a quiet oasis to unwind and encounter nature up close and personal.

Founded in 1989, the Garden boasts more than 2,000 varieties of ornamental plants and several specialty gardens. These include Camellia, Daylily and Shade Gardens, Butterfly Stroll and Children's Garden, and the Heritage Garden with 1886 agricultural structures and a homestead. A favorite location for weddings is the gazebo on the Great Lawn, which bursts with colorful blooms every spring.

Several overlooks provide stunning views of the Cape Fear River and Cross Creek. Pick up a self-guided map at the Visitors Center and enjoy the garden at your own pace.

536 N Eastern Blvd., 910-486-0221
capefearbg.org

DON'T THROW AWAY YOUR SHOT
AT FORT LIBERTY CLAY TARGET CENTER

One of North Carolina's largest shotgun facilities is located just north of Fort Libery (formerly Fort Bragg) in Spring Lake. This world-class facility, which hosts national competitions each year, features 12 competition-level skeet fields, 6 of which are overlaid with competition-level trap fields. The lighted range offers a voice release system for trap, skeet, and 5-stand; 28 partial service RV sites; pro shop; snack bar; and covered pavilion with sound system.

Although it's run by the Fort Liberty Morale, Welfare, and Recreation (MWR) division, the facility is open to the public. All levels of shooters, from beginners to experts, are welcome. Shooters must be eight years or older.

New to the sport? Team members are on hand to provide instructions on the basics, setting everyone up to hit the moving orange target. All necessary equipment can be rented on-site, or you can bring your own.

651 E Manchester Rd., Spring Lake, 910-436-9489
bragg.armymwr.com/programs/clay-target-center

52

TRAVEL TO THE JURASSIC AGE
AT DINOSAUR WORLD

Ever imagined what it would be like to walk among dinosaurs? Wonder no more. Each summer, Dinosaur World at Sweet Valley Ranch provides the opportunity.

Upon arrival, guests take a shuttle ride to the ¼-mile, woodsy and paved Dinosaur Trail, where they encounter more than 40 dinosaurs in a natural habitat. The life-size dinosaurs come to life and move and roar as guests walk by, providing an interactive experience.

Admission to Dinosaur World includes not only the Dinosaur Trail, but the Ice Cave (showcasing Ice Age creatures), Reptile House, Fossil Museum, exotic bird aviary, fossil dig, and a self-guided tour of the 300-acre Sweet Valley Ranch.

In addition to Dinosaur World, Sweet Valley Ranch provides seasonal entertainment throughout the year. Visit their website to learn what is on tap during your visit.

2990 Sunnyside School Rd., 844-622-3276
sweetvalleyranchnc.com

53

DRIVE THROUGH A WINTER WONDERLAND
AT CHRISTMAS IN THE PARK

Every December, Fayetteville-Cumberland Parks & Recreation decorates Arnette Park for the community and its visitors to experience the sights and sounds of the season from the comfort of their car. Christmas in the Park is a combination of holiday-themed displays and natural woodland spanning 100 acres of Arnette Park, which is adjacent to the Cape Fear River.

Tune your radio to the designated station and listen to holiday music while driving along the 1-mile perimeter road. Kids and kids at heart will wonder at the moving and lively displays featuring seasonal favorites such as Frosty, elves, and, of course, Santa. This free show is typically open Sunday through Thursday. However, check the website for dates and times.

This free, community-favorite event typically attracts large crowds. Arrive early to avoid a long wait or plan accordingly.

2165 Wilmington Hwy., 910-433-1547
fcpr.us

54

UNWIND
ALONG THE CAPE FEAR RIVER TRAIL

The Cape Fear River Trail is a 10-foot-wide paved path for walking, running, and nonmotorized transportation. It winds 7 miles one-way and offers spectacular views of the Cape Fear River. More than 1,000 feet of boardwalk takes visitors through the marsh and wetlands along the trail. A favorite feature is a covered bridge.

More than 700 species of plants and trees and 150 species of birds call the region around the trail home. Frogs, lizards, and turtles are common sights. Occasionally, a deer, turkey, or bald eagle are spotted.

The trail is part of the East Coast Greenway, which is being developed as an urban alternative to the Appalachian Trail. The trailhead is at Clark Park.

631 Sherman Dr., 910-433-1579
fcpr.us

TIP

Located off the Cape Fear River Trail is the Cape Fear Mountain Bike Trail. Just over 11 miles, the trail features sections for beginners and more advanced riders. Access is located 1 mile north of Clark Park.

ROOT FOR YOUR FAVORITE DRIVER

AT FAYETTEVILLE MOTOR SPEEDWAY

Built in 1968, Fayetteville Motor Speedway has hosted several noteworthy racers, including Dale Earnhardt, who won twice there in 1978 before launching his full-time NASCAR career.

Today, on most Saturday evenings from March through November, fans pack the stands to watch weekend legends compete on the ¼-mile dirt track. Four standard classes race most nights (602 Late Models, 602 Modifieds, Street Stock, and Legends) along with a traveling series.

Race fanatics, casual fans, and those new to the sport will enjoy an evening at the speedway. Bring lawn chairs or stadium seats, arrive early to watch the qualifiers, and socialize with friends or other race fans. Personal coolers are allowed in the grandstand.

Adult tickets run between $15 and $25. Many discounts are offered, and active-duty service members receive free admission.

3035 Whitman Rd., 910-990-3488
fayettevillemotorspeedway.com

56

SUIT UP
AT BLACK OPS PAINTBALL & AIRSOFT

Two combat veterans established Black Ops Paintball & Airsoft in 2012 with one small woodsball field. Today, it is a 300-acre exciting experience for all skill levels.

Competitions are held on speedball fields, woodsball arenas, hyperball fields, and a mock-up city. Airsoft players can stage at the "Elite Force Pavilion," and then battle in the Tippmann CQB indoor arena and on more than 50 acres of fields.

While paintball and airsoft have some similarities, they are different games. Airsoft is a combat game where players shoot round plastic pellets fired from guns that resemble real firearms. Paintball players shoot paintballs at each other from special paintball guns. Players must be at least 8 to participate in paintball and 12 for airsoft.

Black Ops offers low-impact paintball for anyone 6 and over and Gel Blasters, a no-mess option that shoots small orbeez (tiny squishy bouncy balls), for players 4 and older.

2112 River Rd., 910-876-4444
blackopspaintball.org

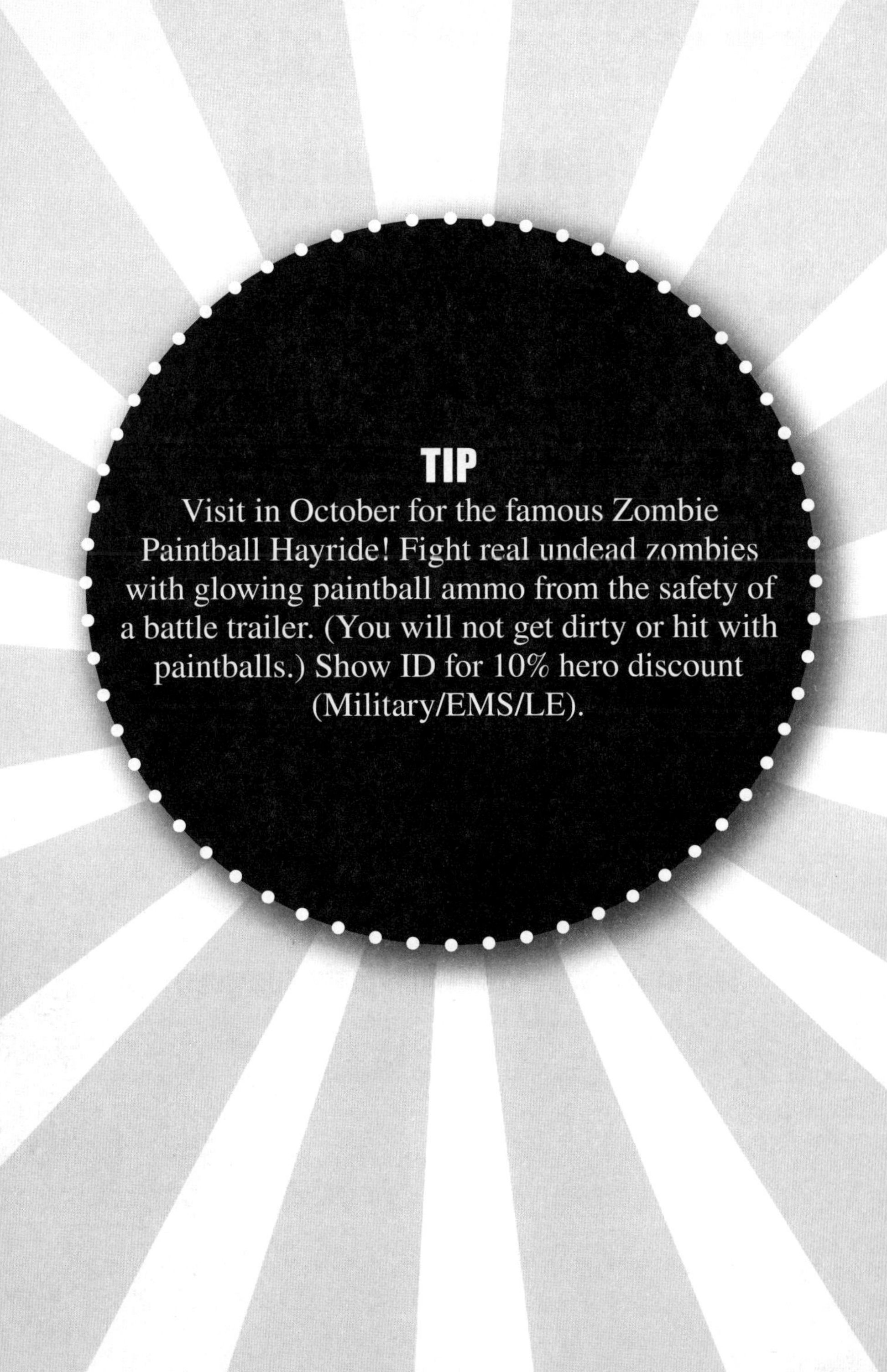

TIP

Visit in October for the famous Zombie Paintball Hayride! Fight real undead zombies with glowing paintball ammo from the safety of a battle trailer. (You will not get dirty or hit with paintballs.) Show ID for 10% hero discount (Military/EMS/LE).

JUMP AROUND
AT JP'S JUMP MASTERS

After her husband, John F. Pettit, a retired Special Forces Medic who had completed two tours in Afghanistan and one in Iraq, died of a heart attack at age 36, Christy Pettit opened JP's Jump Masters in his memory. She envisioned a safe place that people of all ages can play, relax, and even listen to live music. Her dream became reality when the 20,000-square-foot facility opened in early 2018.

About half the facility is dedicated to a trampoline park, which not only has trampolines but also a dodgeball arena, basketball courts, foam pits, and a special area for little jumpers. After burning off energy in the park, guests can grab a gourmet coffee and a snack at JP's large indoor cafe. Be sure to try the authentic New York–style pizza.

A generous arcade wraps up the facility's offerings.

7005 Nexus Ct., 910-223-0200
jpjumpmasters.com

TWO OTHER TRAMPOLINE PARKS IN THE COMMUNITY

DEFY Fayetteville
361 Westwood Shopping Center, 910-302-5400
defy.com/defy-fayetteville

Surge Adventure Park
3333 N Main St., Hope Mills, 910-710-5162
surgefun.com/locations/fayetteville

BREATHE EASIER
AT HOPE MILLS LAKE

Spend a day or even just a few hours relaxing along the water at Hope Mills Lake, and you'll leave refreshed. Pick a nice day, spread out your blanket, and enjoy the ambience. Spend your time fishing, boating, sunbathing, playing beach games, or just relaxing with a good book. A small swimming area is open in the summer.

Arrive in the early morning and catch the kayakers, paddle boarders, and canoers heading out for time on the water. They may be fishing for the latest catch, which can include largemouth bass, bluegill, and channel catfish.

During the warmer months, after a day of fun, cool down with a Snoball from Big T's. It may take you a few minutes to choose a flavor from the panel full of Snoball options.

Boatman Dr., Off N Main St., Hope Mills, 910-424-4555
townofhopemills.com

RUN AWHILE
AT THE FIRECRACKER 4-MILER

The Fayetteville Run Club's Firecracker 4-Miler is as much a part of July 4th in Fayetteville as barbecues and fireworks. People with all levels of experience participate in the run, from serious runners to beginners and even walkers. Most are decked out in their red, white, and blue finest. A 1-mile fun run kicks off just after the 4-miler for attendees who might find the 4-miler daunting. All finishers receive a medal at the finish line.

The course is designed as a historic tour of downtown Fayetteville. It starts and finishes on the streets of Fayetteville at the intersection of Walter and Hillsboro, which is located between the NC State Veterans Park and the Airborne & Special Operations Museum.

Proceeds from the run, which happens on or close to July 4th, benefit a military charity.

100 Hay St.
fayrunclub.org

GET SPOOKED
AT STONEY POINT TRAIL OF TERROR

Stoney Point Fire Department's annual fundraiser, the Stoney Point Trail of Terror, is a highlight of the Halloween season in Fayetteville. New scenes are added each year, meaning the terror-filled wooded trail expands and changes each season. Live actors and state-of-the-art sound, lighting, and environmental effects come together to produce a high-quality haunted experience. Watch for creepy clowns, monsters, zombies, and other terrifying creatures while walking the trail.

Hugely popular, there is typically a wait to walk through the ¾-mile trail—but don't worry! A live band plays each night to entertain patrons waiting to enter the trail, and a stocked concession stand sells snacks. Entirely run by volunteers, all proceeds from the Trail of Terror benefit the Fire Department, which uses funds for lifesaving equipment and continuing education.

7221 Stoney Point Rd., 910-424-0694
undeadfd.com

61

PLAY A ROUND
AT CYPRESS LAKES GOLF COURSE

Cypress Lakes Golf Course, where champion golfers Ray and Marlene Floyd honed their skills, offers golfers a fair and challenging course. A highlight is hole number 9, which is a 160+ yard shot over a pond. On the back nine, players will especially enjoy hole number 11, which is a z-shaped par 5. The final hole is a special challenge with hills, backyards, and water hazards. An elevated green with three levels makes even the best golfer work for their par shot.

The course is set in a panorama of trees, lakes, and streams. The location sets a beautiful background to enjoy while playing.

Practice before your round at the all-grass driving range. Excellent yardage markers help identify the length of your shot. There is also a large practice putting green that mimics the greens on the course.

2126 Cypress Lakes Rd., Hope Mills, 910-483-0359
cypresslakesnc.com

STROLL AWHILE
AT LAKE RIM PARK

Lake Rim Park in western Cumberland County affords families a lot of options for getting active outdoors. It features two playgrounds, picnic areas, ball fields, an aquatic center with slides and other play features, and a dirt walking trail. Access the 1-mile Border Trail from the right parking area. The trail rises with several easy inclines, winds through the wetlands, and continues onto a wooden boardwalk that leads to Bones Creek.

Don't overlook the tar kiln remains. Tar kilns were large outdoor ovens where lightwood was stacked and burned to yield pine tar. Once part of Weed's Lightwood Plant, the remains are one of just a few tangible relics of North Carolina's turpentine industry.

2214 Tar Kiln Dr., 910-433-1018
fcpr.us

TIP

Lake Rim Park is also an ecoEXPLORE Hotspot, a program developed by the NC Arboretum that allows kids to share their observations at ecoexplore.net and earn prizes.

63

PICK YOUR OWN STRAWBERRIES
AT GILLIS HILL ROAD PRODUCE

Each year in April, strawberries ripen on the vine as the temperatures begin to rise. Folks who enjoy the taste of freshly picked strawberries will find plenty of places to get their fill. Several local farmers open their fields for visitors to pick their own.

Family-owned Gillis Hill Road Produce offers daily picking during strawberry season, typically mid-April through the end of May. After picking their fill of strawberries, guests are invited to shop at the produce market, which sells freshly grown produce from Gillis Hill Farm, a ninth-generation farm in Western Cumberland County.

Gillis Hill Road Produce hosts special events throughout the year and is most active during the fall, when the corn maze and pumpkin patch are open.

2899 Gillis Hill Rd., 910-308-9342
facebook.com/gillishillroadproduce

TWO OTHER GREAT LOCATIONS TO PICK STRAWBERRIES

Bunce Brothers Farm
6267 Blake Rd., Stedman, 910-483-5007
facebook.com/buncebrothersfarms

Canady Farm
1426 John McMillan Rd., Hope Mills, 910-624-2959
facebook.com/canadyfarm

64

REACH NEW HEIGHTS
AT THE CLIMBING PLACE

Designed in the early 1990s, The Climbing Place (TCP) is North Carolina's oldest climbing gym, and many climbers say it's also the best. TCP continuously adds new walls and features to meet the evolving needs of climbers.

Beginners to experts can challenge themselves at the facility, which houses 20,000 square feet of climbing walls that include top rope, bouldering, top out, ledge, traverse, Ninja Warrior, obstacles, slacklines, military ropes, campus boards, and a cargo net. For advanced climbers, TCP offers more than 50 top ropes as well as lead climbing. Climbers can bring their own gear or rent gear on-site.

Caring and professional staff offer belay classes, technique classes, and advanced climbing classes. They are on hand to answer all your questions. Additionally, a retail store carries climbing equipment. The gym is open Monday through Saturday, and walk-ins are welcome.

436 W Russell St., 910-486-9638
theclimbingplace.com

Airborne Special Operations Museum lobby,
courtesy of DistiNCtly Fayetteville

CULTURE AND HISTORY

WALK THROUGH MILITARY HISTORY AT THE US ARMY AIRBORNE & SPECIAL OPERATIONS MUSEUM

Not only is the lobby of the US Army Airborne & Special Operations Museum architecturally stunning, it also sets the stage for what visitors will encounter in the museum. Two paratroopers hang from the ceiling on deployed parachutes. One represents a modern-day paratrooper, the other, a 1940s, first-generation World War II–era soldier.

Upon entering the galleries, guests take a walk-through time, starting with the first airborne jumps in 1940, and ending with the Global War on Terror. One-third of the space is dedicated to World War II. In addition to the retired military equipment on display, the facility incorporates plenty of smaller details such as personal stories, photographs, equipment, and locally owned uniforms.

Visitors can also enjoy the Pritzker Motion Simulator, which is a 24-seat platform that moves up in concert with two films designated to simulate parachuting and helicopter flights at treetop level. The "ride" gives the viewer the opportunity to immerse themselves in high-speed military action.

100 Bragg Blvd., 910-643-2778
asomf.org

TIP
Get a picture in front of the iconic statue *Iron Mike*. He stands in tribute to all Airborne troopers and is one of the top places for pictures in Fayetteville.

66

REMEMBER FOUR-LEGGED HEROES

AT CONSTANT VIGILANCE

Constant Vigilance, the first memorial in the world dedicated to special operations canines killed in action, stands on the grounds of the US Army Airborne & Special Operations Museum.

The bronze statue depicts a life-size Belgian Malinois in full combat gear. The Belgian Malinois often serves in special forces units because of its strength, easy trainability, and natural instincts to do the job. The statue memorializes dogs from the United States, the United Kingdom, and Australia killed in the line of duty since 9/11. In front of the sculpture, granite paver stones list the name, date of birth, and death for each canine.

The inscription at the base reads "CONSTANT VIGILANCE The bond between a SOF handler & his K9 is eternal; Trusting each other in a nameless language. Here we honor our SOF K9's that have paid the ultimate price."

100 Bragg Blvd., 910-643-2778
asomf.org

TRAVEL THE WORLD
AT THE INTERNATIONAL FOLK FESTIVAL

Thanks to nearby Fort Liberty (formerly Fort Bragg), the largest army base in the United States (by population), the Fayetteville community enjoys an international diversity. This diversity is evident in the annual International Folk Festival, held the last weekend in September in downtown Fayetteville.

The two-day festival starts with the Parade of Nations, in which more than 30 cultural groups parade in traditional costumes and often offer the music and dance from their region. A kids area includes arts, crafts, and educational content to help younger attendees explore other cultures. The festival also features an arts market, an area for nonprofits, and live entertainment on several stages throughout the weekend.

A festival favorite is an International Café, which offers a rare opportunity to sample food from a range of cuisines in one location.

Downtown Fayetteville, 910-323-1776
theartscouncil.com

TIP

Plan to spend several hours at the International Folk Festival. With so much to see and do, you won't want to miss any of it.

EMBRACE A FRIGHT-FREE, FAMILY-FRIENDLY HALLOWEEN

AT THE CAPE FEAR "BOOTANICAL" GARDEN

Event planners at the 77-acre botanical garden take their special event decorating seriously and spend weeks preparing the garden for an upcoming event. Halloween at the "Bootanical" Garden features hundreds of jack-o'-lanterns, lights, and luminaries along the garden trails.

Put the kids in costume and hand them a flashlight to help navigate the beautifully lit trails. Arts and crafts, special activities, and trick or treating stations line the lit pathway for plenty of family-friendly fun. Lawn games and music round out the daily activities. Refreshments are available for purchase. Halloween at the Bootanical Garden is a multiday event, and the first night of the event is often dog friendly. On this evening, dog treats are offered to our four-legged family members.

536 N Eastern Blvd., 910-486-0221
capefearbg.org

STROLL THE STREETS
AT FOURTH FRIDAY

On the Fourth Friday of every month from March to October, downtown Fayetteville comes alive with artists, performances, vendors, and attractions from 6 p.m. to 9 p.m.

Join the vibe and experience Fourth Friday as you walk through the crowded streets to find belly dancers, whittlers, painters, martial arts presentations, a variety of musicians, and vendors displaying their hand-crafted wares. Visit downtown art galleries for the latest exhibit openings. Downtown restaurants, coffee shops, and stores stay busy with special promotions and extended hours. Beer drinkers can grab a local brew at one of two breweries in the downtown district.

Once a year, Fourth Friday includes a family-friendly scavenger hunt with great prizes. The best part of Fourth Friday? It is one of Fayetteville's many free events. Fourth Friday is hosted by the Cool Spring Downtown District.

222 Hay St., 910-223-1089
visitdowntownfayetteville.com

DISCOVER FAYETTEVILLE'S ROOTS
AT THE FAYETTEVILLE HISTORY MUSEUM

Prior to the development of Fort Liberty (formerly Fort Bragg) in the early 20th century, Fayetteville was a key city in North Carolina. Goods, which had traveled up the Cape Fear River by steamship from the Wilmington port, were distributed throughout the state by coach, train, and even, for a period, plank roads. Travel to and from Fayetteville was key to its development as a trade center. The Fayetteville History Museum interprets this early history of Fayetteville through the 20th century. Favorite spots include the steamboats and the recreated Station Agent's Office. (The steamboat section provides the tidbit that steamboat schedules were merely "suggestions.") Additionally, special exhibits rotate throughout the year.

The building itself is a marvel. The museum is located in the 1890 Cape Fear and Yadkin Valley Railroad Depot.

325 Franklin St., 910-433-1547
fcpr.us

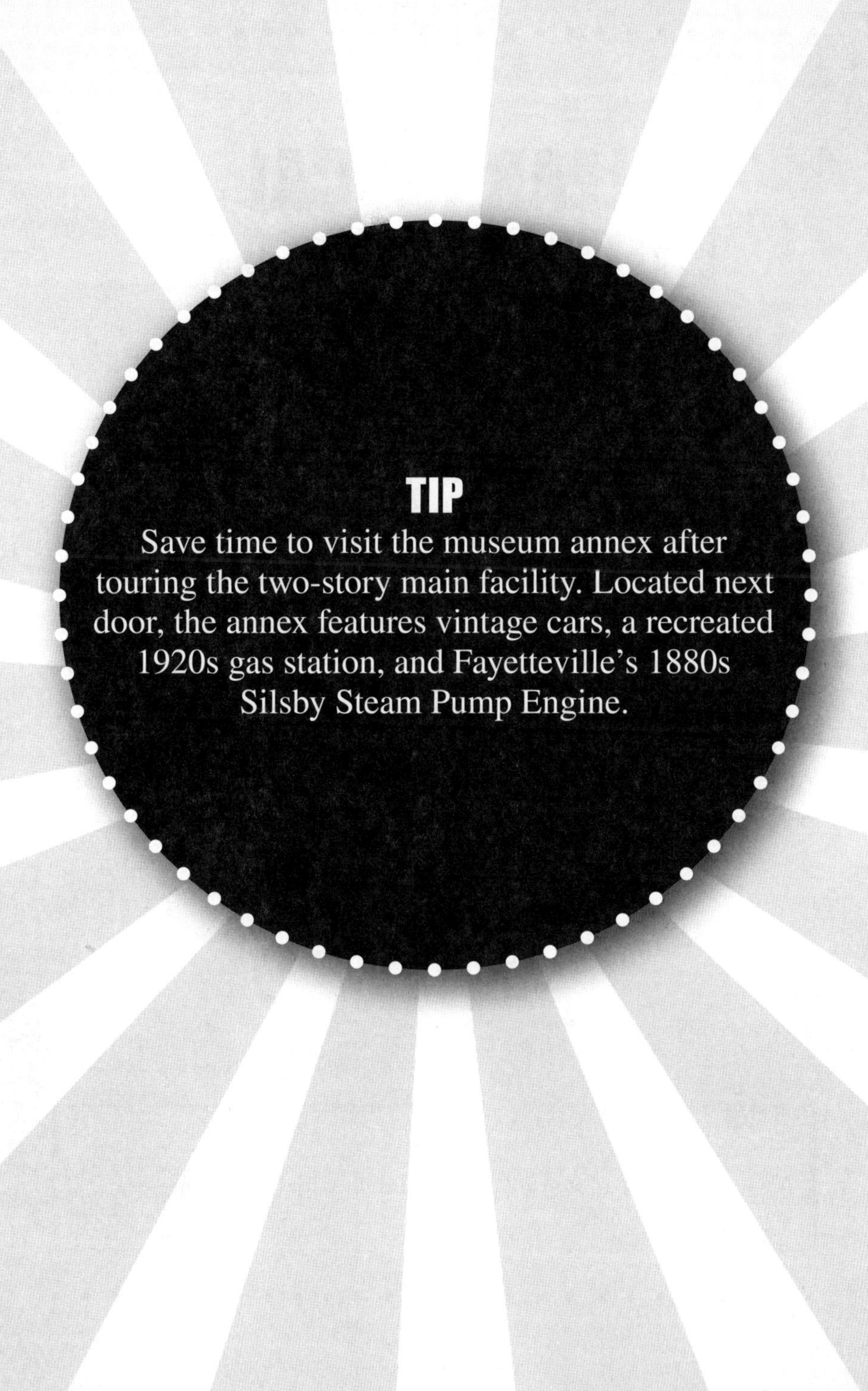

TIP

Save time to visit the museum annex after touring the two-story main facility. Located next door, the annex features vintage cars, a recreated 1920s gas station, and Fayetteville's 1880s Silsby Steam Pump Engine.

71

LEARN LOCAL FARMING HISTORY
AT GILLIS HILL FARM

Gillis Hill Farm embraces its history as a centuries-old working farm. The family's story started with the arrival of Malcolm Gillis in the early 18th century. Today, members of Malcolm's family still work on the same land. Many farm guests start their visit by purchasing fresh, homemade ice cream and enjoying the sweet treat stretched out on the rocking chairs that line the farmhouse porch. Afterward, guests are invited on a self-guided tour of the farm where they can see restored farm buildings, view and feed the farm animals, relax on the swings and play yard games, or watch the kids burn off their energy in the sand play area. The farm is open April through October.

2701 Gillis Hill Rd., 910-867-2350
gillishillfarm.com

TIP

In season, be sure to stop at Gillis Hill Produce for fresh veggies and locally made goodies.

HONOR THE SACRIFICES OF ALL NORTH CAROLINA VETERANS

AT NORTH CAROLINA VETERANS PARK

The first park dedicated to honoring North Carolina veterans from all branches of service stands in downtown Fayetteville across from the Airborne & Special Operations Museum.

The park includes an arch dedicated to each branch of service, sculptures made from salvaged military equipment, lovely water features highlighting inspiring quotes, and an Oath Wall. On the Oath Wall, four sculpted hands from veterans in each of North Carolina's 100 counties pay tribute to all the veterans that took the oath to serve.

Don't miss the memorable exhibits in the visitor center. A chandelier made of 33,500 dog tags hangs from the ceiling. A somber display features dog tags from every North Carolina service member killed in action from World War II to the present day. Separated by conflict, each dog tag is inscribed with the name of the service member. It's not unusual to find visitors searching for a specific name.

300 Bragg Blvd., 910-433-1547
fcpr.us

STEP INTO FAYETTEVILLE'S REVOLUTIONARY WAR–ERA HISTORY

AT LIBERTY POINT

On June 20, 1775, a year before the Declaration of Independence was signed, a group of local patriots signed a declaration of freedom commonly called "The Liberty Point Resolves." This moment is memorialized on a granite sculpture at Liberty Point in downtown Fayetteville. Liberty Point is a vestige of early street patterns with its triangular plot.

The 55 local dignitaries that signed the document pledged to "go forth and be ready to sacrifice our lives and fortunes to secure her freedom and safety."

The original document is preserved in the Southern Historical Collection at the University of Chapel Hill. Periodically, the document is put on display at the Fayetteville History Museum.

Person and Bow Streets, Downtown Fayetteville

For more on the era's Revolutionary War history, explore the American Independence Trail, which is offered on distinctlyfayettevillenc.com. Many of the sites are within walking distance in the downtown region.

DIVE INTO LIFE IN THE EARLY 20TH CENTURY
AT THE 1897 E. A. POE HOUSE

The 1897 E. A. Poe House was the home of affluent businessman and local brickmaker E. A. Poe (not the author!) and his family for almost 100 years. When Mr. Poe's last daughter died in 1988, she donated the house to the Museum of the Cape Fear Historical Complex, which is located next door. The museum facility is a branch of the North Carolina Museum of History.

A tour of the home sheds light on life and traditions in the early 20th century. Don't miss dual light fixtures for both gas and electric, hair collectors and hair jewelry, the children's homework, calling card collectors, and photographs of the family. Guided tours are available throughout the week. Be sure to look up during your visit so you don't miss the beautiful ceilings and woodwork.

801 Arsenal Ave., 910-500-4240
museumofthecapefear.ncdcr.gov

TIP

Plan a visit during the Christmas season when the house is festively decorated and the tours feature Christmas traditions of the era.

STOP AND SMELL THE ROSES

AT FAYETTEVILLE ROSE GARDEN

For more than 50 years, the Fayetteville Rose Garden has provided a serene spot to relax and soak in the serenity of thousands of rose blooms. Today, the garden boasts nearly 1,000 bushes in three dozen varieties. These include some of the original plantings. In the midst of the garden are benches that surround a lovely fountain.

The garden is located on the grounds of Fayetteville Technical Community College (FTCC) and is maintained collaboratively by FTCC and the Fayetteville Rose Society. The maintenance team aims to display roses that will appeal to the casual observer and the discerning rose enthusiast.

The garden can be reserved for special events, and it's a site for many local weddings.

2201 Hull Rd., 910-678-8228

76

ENCOUNTER ARTISTIC EXPRESSION AT THE ARTS CENTER GALLERY

Throughout the year, the Arts Center Gallery hosts rotating exhibits in their downtown Fayetteville gallery. Although the gallery occasionally hosts national exhibits, it typically focuses on North Carolina artists who work in all types of media.

Past exhibits include a juried exhibit titled "10:10:10", which encouraged unconventional artistic architectural expressions of the artist's vision; "I Am Somebody: Faces of Homelessness," a visual exhibition; and "Vanguard Social: Visions of Southern Queer Resistance," which showcased 20 Southern QTBIPOC artists. A local favorite is "PWC Public Works." In this exhibit, residents of all abilities, ages, and backgrounds submit their work for display and the chance to win a People's Choice Award.

Admission to the Arts Center Gallery, which is in a renovated 1910 post office, is always free. Visit the website to see the upcoming exhibit schedule.

301 Hay St., 910-323-1776
theartscouncil.com

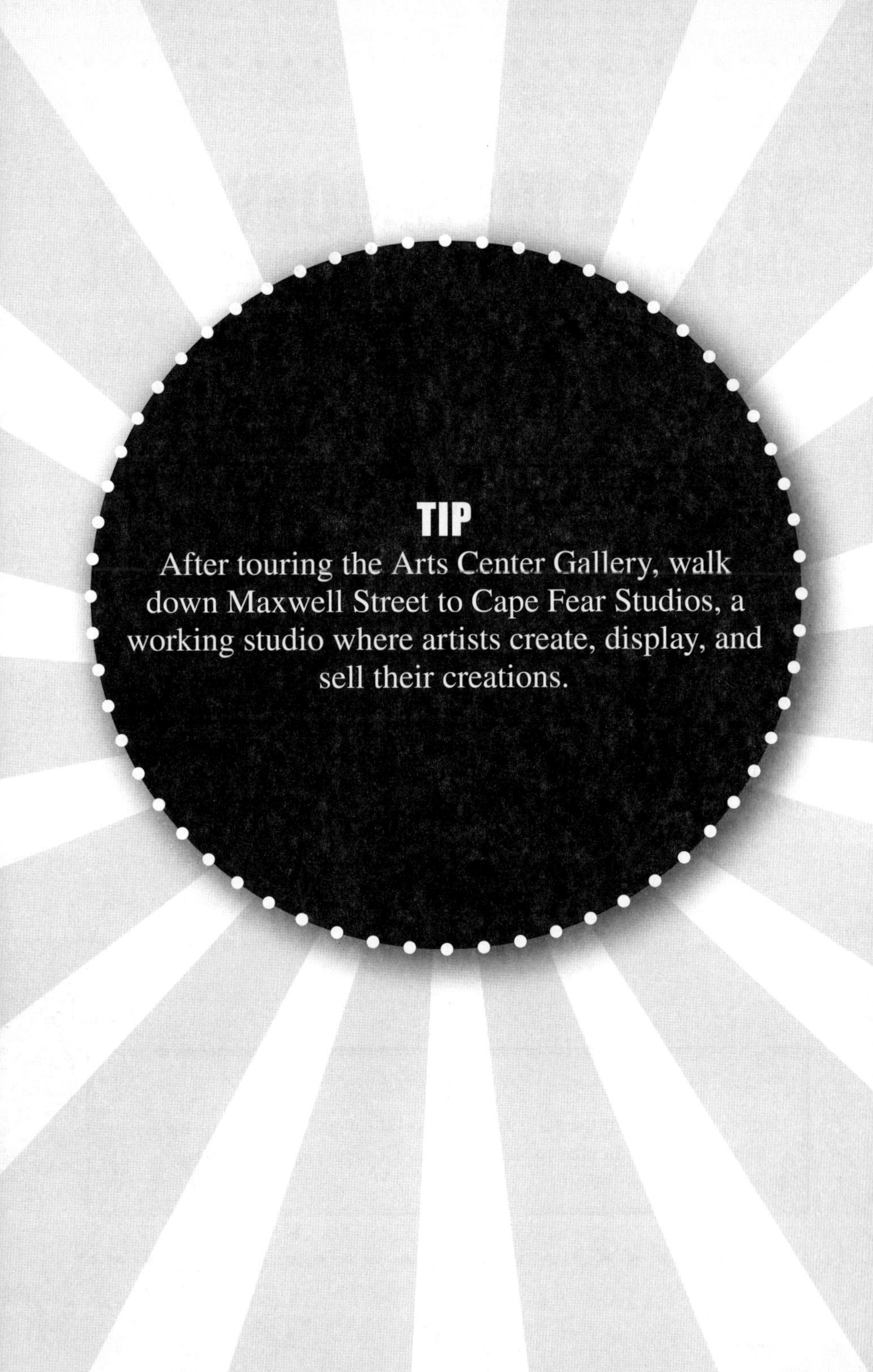

TIP

After touring the Arts Center Gallery, walk down Maxwell Street to Cape Fear Studios, a working studio where artists create, display, and sell their creations.

STEP TO THE SPOOKY SIDE
AND VISIT CROSS CREEK CEMETERY #1

Established in 1785, Cross Creek Cemetery is the oldest Cemetery in Fayetteville. It is home to more than 1,100 graves dated between 1786 and 1964, including some of the prominent early residents of Fayetteville such as Robert Adams, Duncan McRae, John Sandford, and Andrew Broadfoot.

Walk among the graves, and you may notice some smooth, beautiful stones that read perfectly after more than 150 years. Chances are that stone was created by Fayetteville resident George Lauder, known as North Carolina's most prominent stone mason of the 19th century. Lauder often signed his stones with "Lauder." For an example of his work, look for the grave of Samuel H. Pemberton, who died on July 1, 1856. Lauder is also buried at Cross Creek Cemetery #1.

Cool Spring and Grove Streets, 910-433-1457

TIP

Lauder also created the tall stone memorial toward the back of the cemetery. It is dedicated to the unnamed Confederate and Union soldiers buried at the site.

CELEBRATE
AT THE AREA'S LARGEST JULY 4TH CELEBRATION!

Is there a better way to commemorate the birthday of America than with the military who dedicate themselves to its service? On July 4th, civilian and military families gather at Fort Liberty (formerly Fort Bragg) Main Post Parade Field to mark the fourth with activities from midafternoon until dark when the area's best firework display lights the sky.

The schedule typically includes a performance by the 82nd Airborne Band, a parachute jump (weather permitting) and flag ceremony, performances by a regional band and a national act, a kiddie zone, and food vendors. The day ends after the fireworks.

This special event is free and open to civilians and the military. Check the website for a schedule of events and instructions for civilian access to Fort Liberty.

Fort Liberty Main Post Parade Field
bragg.armymwr.com

TIP

The event is hugely popular. Leave early to allow time for parking and access. Check the website for parking maps.

EXAMINE EDUCATION HISTORY
AT FAYETTEVILLE STATE UNIVERSITY

It's a little-known fact that Fayetteville is home to the second oldest state-supported school in North Carolina. Fayetteville State University was originally founded in 1867 as the Howard School for African Americans. It was named after General O. O. Howard, director of the Freedmen's Bureau, when seven black men purchased the land for $136. In 1877, the Howard School was designated as the first State Colored Normal School to educate African American teachers. In 1939, it became a four-year college, and, in 1972, it became part of the UNC System. Prominent past presidents include E. E. Smith and Charles Chesnutt, the first prominent African American author. On the grounds, visitors can view the E. E. Smith monument, explore the archives at the Chesnutt Library, view historical buildings and original college gates, tour the art gallery, or attend one of the cultural events held year-round.

1200 Murchison Rd., 910-672-1111
uncfsu.edu

VISIT A LIVING MILITARY TRIBUTE AT FIELD OF HONOR

For nearly two months each year, hundreds of flags line the Parade Field at the US Army Airborne & Special Operations Museum in perfect formation during Fayetteville's Field of Honor. Each flag in the breathtaking display tells a story by identifying the person who sponsored the flag and the flag honoree. Flags can be purchased to honor a service member who has died, a veteran, or a current service member from any branch of service.

The effect of hundreds of flags blowing in the breezes is stunning. Knowing there is a story behind every flag in Field of Honor makes the experience truly moving. Organizers welcome service members, families, residents, and visitors who wish to experience and capture this living display of heroism. Don't miss it.

100 Bragg Blvd.
asomf.org

81

WALK WITH THE ROCKEFELLERS

AT CARVERS CREEK STATE PARK

Visitors to Carvers Creek State Park can enjoy a leisurely stroll along easy trails that lead to Long Valley Farm, the winter estate of James Stillman Rockefeller, which sits on a 100-acre millpond. The beautiful home is on the National Register of Historic Places. Visitors can look toward the dam and see the pavilion, which used to be a sawmill in the 1800s, and the grist mill, which played a vital role in utilizing waterpower in the early 1900s.

Carvers Creek State Park is home to the rare Longleaf Pine Ecosystem, which is home to endangered species, including the red-cockaded woodpecker. Nearby Fort Liberty (formerly Fort Bragg) won several environmental awards for its conservation efforts, in part because of its protection of the red-cockaded woodpecker.

2505 Long Valley Rd., Spring Lake, 910-436-4681
ncparks.gov

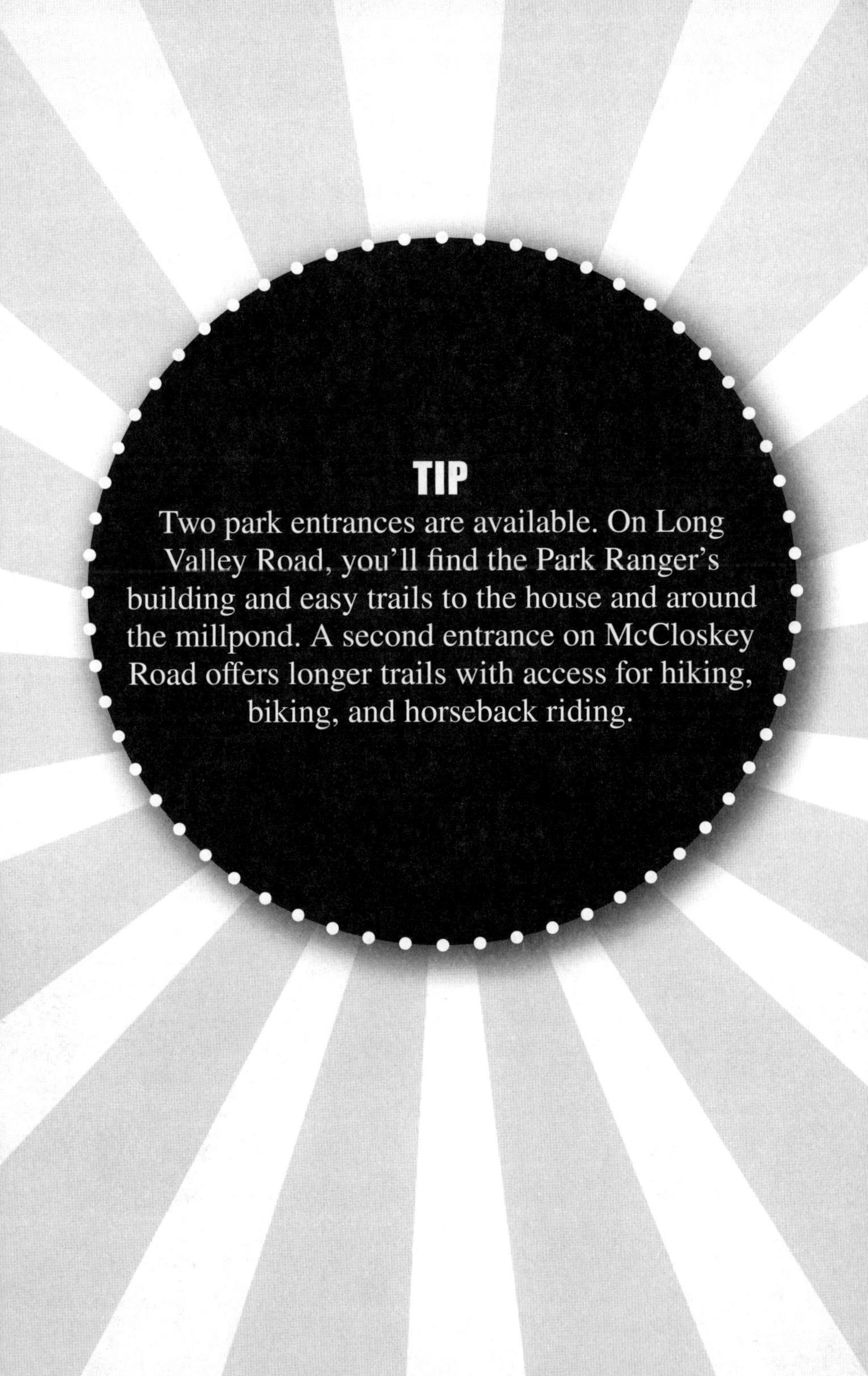

TIP

Two park entrances are available. On Long Valley Road, you'll find the Park Ranger's building and easy trails to the house and around the millpond. A second entrance on McCloskey Road offers longer trails with access for hiking, biking, and horseback riding.

A Bit of Carolina, courtesy of A Bit of Carolina

SHOPPING AND FASHION

82

SNAG INEXPENSIVE ACTIVEWEAR
AT SOFFE OUTLET STORE

M. J. Soffe's legacy began in 1946 when his company began producing apparel for military exchanges and college bookstores. Since that time, the Fayetteville company has expanded its focus to include activewear for all types of athletes and exercise. Shop the outlet for retail products at a much lower price point. Military, university, and cheer products are widely available as are products specifically for men, women, and children. Seconds are also often available in bins at the store.

Additionally, Soffe periodically holds a warehouse sale. During this sale, one part of the warehouse is stuffed full of bins of all types of products sorted by type and size for $1 to $5. Shoppers who don't mind a minor imperfection can find great bargains.

1 Soffe Dr., 910-483-1776
soffe.com

SATISFY YOUR SENSES
AT BATH SNOB

Enter Bath Snob, and you'll leave feeling like family. The ladies at Bath Snob take the time to talk about their products and help you sample your options. At any time, the store will carry a variety of soaps, sugar scrubs, body butter, shower steamers, hand cream, bath bombs, and candles.

Shoppers sensitive to fragrances won't have issues with the Bath Snob products—every product is all-natural and handmade in-house without any harsh chemicals. Bath Snob patrons can rely on the staff to help pick the right product for their needs.

If you like what you find at the store but can't visit regularly—not to worry. You can order online.

So, stop by, pick up some locally produced products, and make new friends.

3505 N Main St., Hope Mills, 910-568-3238
bathsnob.com

84

SEARCH FOR SOUTHERN FAVORITES
AT THE PILGRIM GIFTS

A 50-year staple for gift shopping in Fayetteville, The Pilgrim offers a range of gift products with a southern flare.

Looking for a North Carolina–themed gift? You'll find North Carolina food products, clothing, local artwork, jewelry, and handbags at The Pilgrim. A display of small, colorful tiles is particularly meaningful. After her sister died of brain cancer, Laura Harsant Reeves found her sister's journals filled with inspirational sayings and quotes. She began painting the quotes on colorful tiles to work through her grief.

In addition to North Carolina–themed products, The Pilgrim also sells Vera Bradley, Hobo Purses, Simon Sebbag, Lilly Pulitzer, Cotton Colors, Cat Studio, Care's Coasters, Radko, and Charleston Shoes.

A bonus for shopping at The Pilgrim—every purchase qualifies for free gift wrapping.

160 Westwood Shopping Ctr., 910-867-9750

GRAB THE PERFECT GIFT
AT THE FRONT PORCH SOUTHERN DECOR

If you enjoy shopping for homemade products, make time to visit The Front Porch Southern Decor.

Most of the goods are handmade by the owners or other local vendors. Owners strive to offer products that will extend southern hospitality such as wreaths, door hangers, jewelry, clothes, refinished furniture, decorations, food, and more. Christmas is a great time to visit—the store is filled with homemade ornaments and decorations. You'll be sure to find something for almost everyone on your list.

From the outside of the store, the size is deceiving. The small storefront extends backward with a variety of rooms dedicated to types of products such as clothing, food, Christmas, and housewares.

Located just off Trade Street in Hope Mills, in an old mill house, The Front Porch Southern Decor provides a nearly perfect small-town shopping experience.

5548 Trade St., Hope Mills, 910-964-4336
thefrontporchsoutherndecor.com

PAMPER YOUR PUP
AT WOOF GANG BAKERY

Walk through the door at Woof Gang Bakery, and you'll be drawn to the table full of treats that look like they are fresh from a fancy bakery. But these aren't people treats—they're pup treats. There are so many to choose from, you may have trouble making your selection. Two popular fall items are Pumpkin Spice Latte cookies and dried pumpkin sticks.

Although Woof Gang Bakery is part of a national chain, it feels like a neighborhood store. The staff loves to get to know two- and four-legged visitors and is on hand to make recommendations.

The store also carries a range of grain-free pet food, gourmet dog treats, leads, toys, accessories, and more. Should you find fido in need of grooming, you are in luck. Woof Gang Bakery grooms dogs six days a week.

1216 Fort Bragg Rd., 910-860-1200
woofgangbakery.com

MEET THE COMMUNITY
AT LeCLAIR'S GENERAL STORE

LeClair's General Store is not the general store you remember from TV or movies.

The store stocks unique and higher-end products chosen with care, and they are sold in a stunning storefront designed with rustic elegance. If the store's design impresses you—it should. The owner, Patrick LeClair, used to work as a store designer for Ralph Lauren.

LeClair's also sells local and North Carolina beer and wine, pastries, local art, and fresh coffee.

While the products are different from other general stores of the past, LeClair's is similar in one respect: it serves as a meeting place in its community. On any Saturday, you'll see visitors having a coffee, grabbing a quick bite, and having a chat with friends. Seats are located strategically throughout the store. Many regular patrons have a coffee cup that stays in the store. Check out the display behind the register.

1212 Fort Bragg Rd., 910-491-1060
leclairsgeneralstore.com

88

STIR YOUR SENSES
AT HUMMINGBIRD CANDLE COMPANY

Indulge in some self-care and fun, and create a candle all your own at Hummingbird Candle company. During your candle-making experience, the chandlers (candlemakers) guide you throughout the experience of creating your own 9-ounce coconut-oil luxury candle. In the process, you will explore a scent library of more than 30 scents.

Expect lots of laughter, whether you attend with one or a larger group. You are welcome to bring your favorite beverage to enjoy while exploring candle options. While walk-ins are welcome, reservations are recommended.

No time to create a candle? Stop in and browse. Seasonal candles, accessories from women-owned businesses, and candle accessories are for sale.

This Black and woman-owned business made an impression on Fayetteville in three short years and opened a second permanent shop and a temporary pop-up shop in different North Carolina cities.

240 Hay St., 910-223-6247
hummingbirdcandleco.com

89

BROWSE NORTH CAROLINA GIFTS
AT A BIT OF CAROLINA

You don't have to travel the state of North Carolina to find items from around the state, but you do have to stop in at A Bit of Carolina in downtown Fayetteville.

Souvenir shoppers will enjoy North Carolina T-shirts, key chains, magnets, hats, and other traditional souvenir items from North Carolina and Fayetteville. The store's magic lies in the items from more than 60 local consigners—both food vendors and artisans. Shop handmade jewelry, bags, gourmet cookies, crochet hats, hair bows and ribbons, coasters, signs, and baskets—all made locally. Inventory changes often so no two visits to A Bit of Carolina are the same.

Should you need a gift basket, A Bit of Carolina is the best. Stop by for a perfect Carolina-themed basket filled with treats from around the state.

306 Hay St., 910-551-6537
abitofcarolina.com

90

CROSS ITEMS OFF YOUR HOLIDAY LIST
AT HOLLY DAY FAIR

With more than 22,000 attendees and 150 vendors, the Holly Day Fair is one of the largest craft shows in North Carolina. Vendors apply nearly a year early for a coveted spot at the 55-year-old show, which is held over 4 days in early November at the Crown Complex.

Be sure to have your shopping list in hand. More than 80,000 sq. ft. are packed full of unique homemade and handcrafted specialty holiday goods for show and sale. Expect to find holiday decorations, handmade crafts, stylish jewelry and clothes, children's toys, specialty food items, wine, and more. Holly Day Fair is an annual fundraiser for the Junior League of Fayetteville.

1960 Coliseum Dr., 910-323-5509
hollydayfair.com

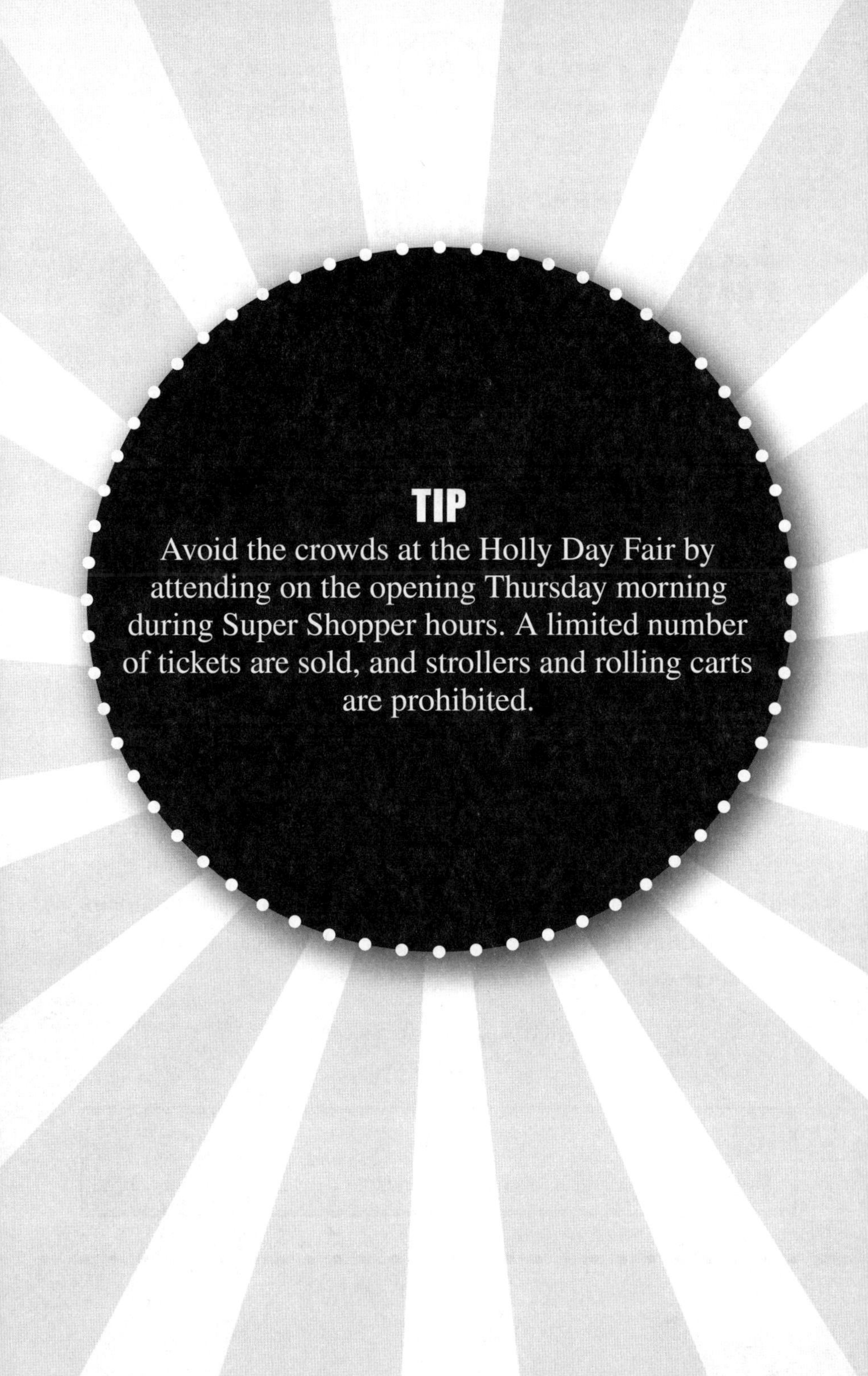

TIP

Avoid the crowds at the Holly Day Fair by attending on the opening Thursday morning during Super Shopper hours. A limited number of tickets are sold, and strollers and rolling carts are prohibited.

FIND FARM FRESH PRODUCTS AT THE DOWNTOWN MARKET OF FAYETTEVILLE

Farmers markets are great, but they aren't open year-round. The Downtown Market of Fayetteville solves that problem. Throughout the year, The Downtown Market works directly with farmers, producers, and artisans to offer farm-fresh and locally produced meats, milk, veggies, drinks, pastries, honey, chocolates, dog treats, flowers, cheese, and more. The store is open Tuesday through Saturday.

If all of that wasn't enough of a reason to stop by The Downtown Market, Benny the Milk Dog is usually in the store greeting customers and accepting pets and love. Benny became "The Milk Dog" because he accompanies his "mom" on daily milk delivery runs. That's right, The Downtown Market delivers milk and other produce items every day to homes and businesses. Visit their website for details.

325 Blount St., 919-349-6062
ncmilkman.com

TIP

The Downtown Market is also a florist, and they deliver fresh blooms daily.

92

GRAB YOUR NEXT GREAT READ

AT CITY CENTER GALLERY & BOOKS

In the heart of downtown Fayetteville, City Center Gallery & Books is a book collector's dream. This used bookstore carries thousands of contemporary and vintage books at a great price. Plan to spend time exploring this store, which is in a beautifully restored circa 1890 building. The ambiance is perfect.

The store is also known for its collection of local artists' work for show and sale. It is the exclusive source for original art and limited editions by the late artist Bob Rector, including classic automobiles, World War II airplanes, and historic downtown buildings. They also carry a collection of photographs, reproductions, and note cards of historic Downtown Fayetteville by award-winning local photographers and artists. Various artists are featured throughout the year.

112 Hay St., 910-678-8899
citycentergallery.com

TIP

Watch their calendar for book signings, author talks, and other special events, which are held throughout the year.

93

LOVE LOCAL ART
AT CAPE FEAR STUDIOS

Stop by this nonprofit art gallery and working studio, and you may spy artists at work producing their next masterpiece. Cape Fear Studios is home to a collective group of artists producing, displaying, and selling their creations.

Visitors are welcome to explore not only the main gallery, which holds paintings, photographs, sculptures, pottery, wood, and glass art created by regional artists, but also each artist's studio to see works in progress.

This artists' collective also showcases local, state, and nationally recognized artists in their main gallery throughout the year. The exhibits often open on Fayetteville's monthly Fourth Friday event, with artist talks and presentations.

Throughout the year, Cape Fear Studios offers classes and workshops such as photography, ceramics, pottery, drawing, and watercolors. Some are one-day sessions, whereas others are several weeks long. Select your session to learn from a local artist.

148 Maxwell St., 910-433-2986
capefearstudios.com

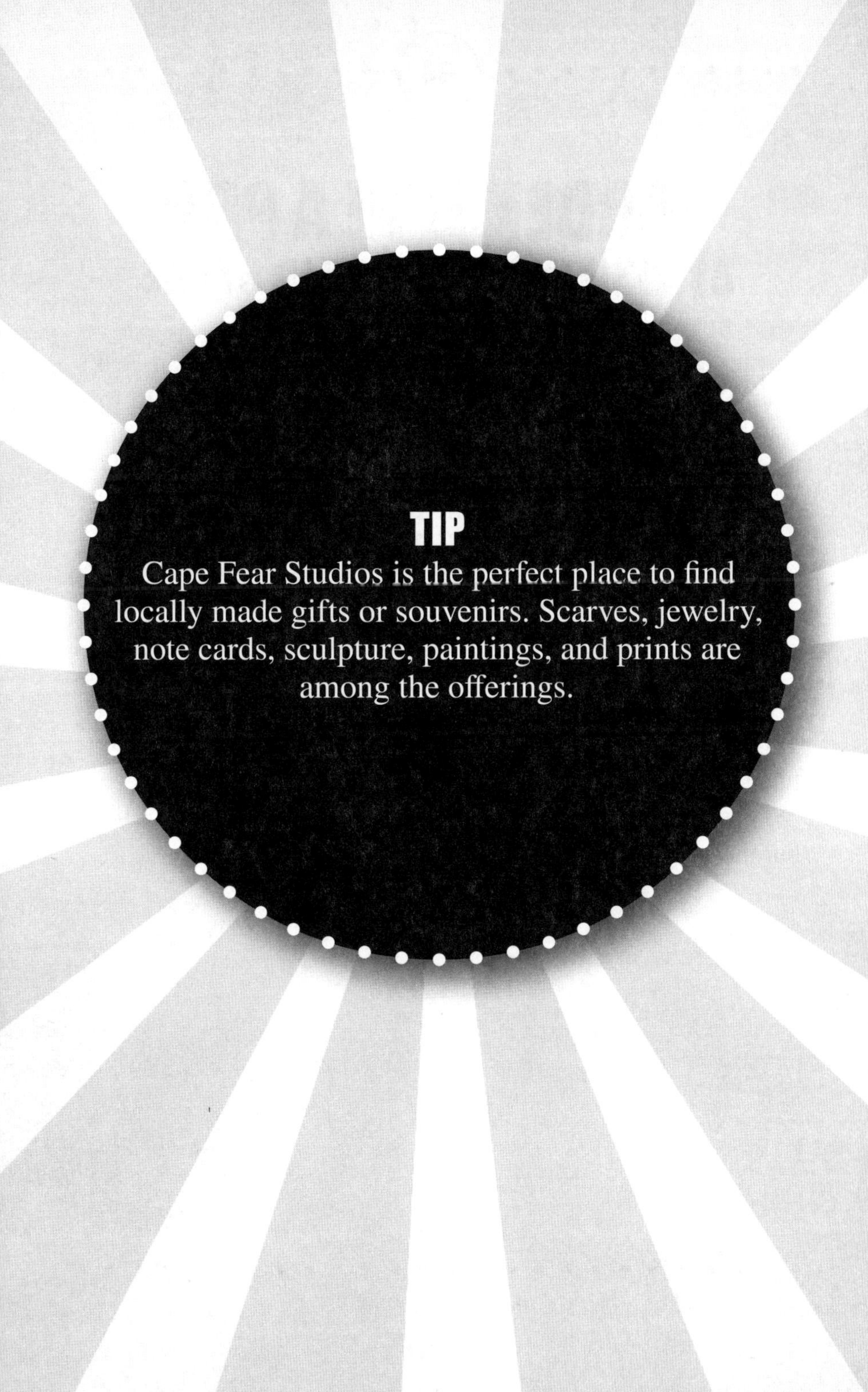
TIP
Cape Fear Studios is the perfect place to find locally made gifts or souvenirs. Scarves, jewelry, note cards, sculpture, paintings, and prints are among the offerings.

94

GARDEN LIKE A PRO
BY VISITING BELL'S SEED STORE

Local gardeners, landscapers, and lawn lovers count on Bell's Seed Store staff to answer their questions and point them to a solution. They also depend on Bell's to carry all the goods they need to keep their lawn, patio, and garden looking lovely.

Having served the community since 1918, it is safe to say that the family-owned Bell's store is an institution. Bell's fills two large buildings, and their product selection seems endless. One building houses home, garden, and patio decorative items, and all your needs for grilling. In the other, find seeds, bulbs, pesticides, gardening and landscaping equipment, and more. Between the buildings, walk among Bell's selection of vegetables, flowers, plants, trees, and shrubs.

When you leave, don't forget to pick up your free Bell's Seed bumper sticker.

230 E Russell St., 910-483-8400
bellsseedstore.com

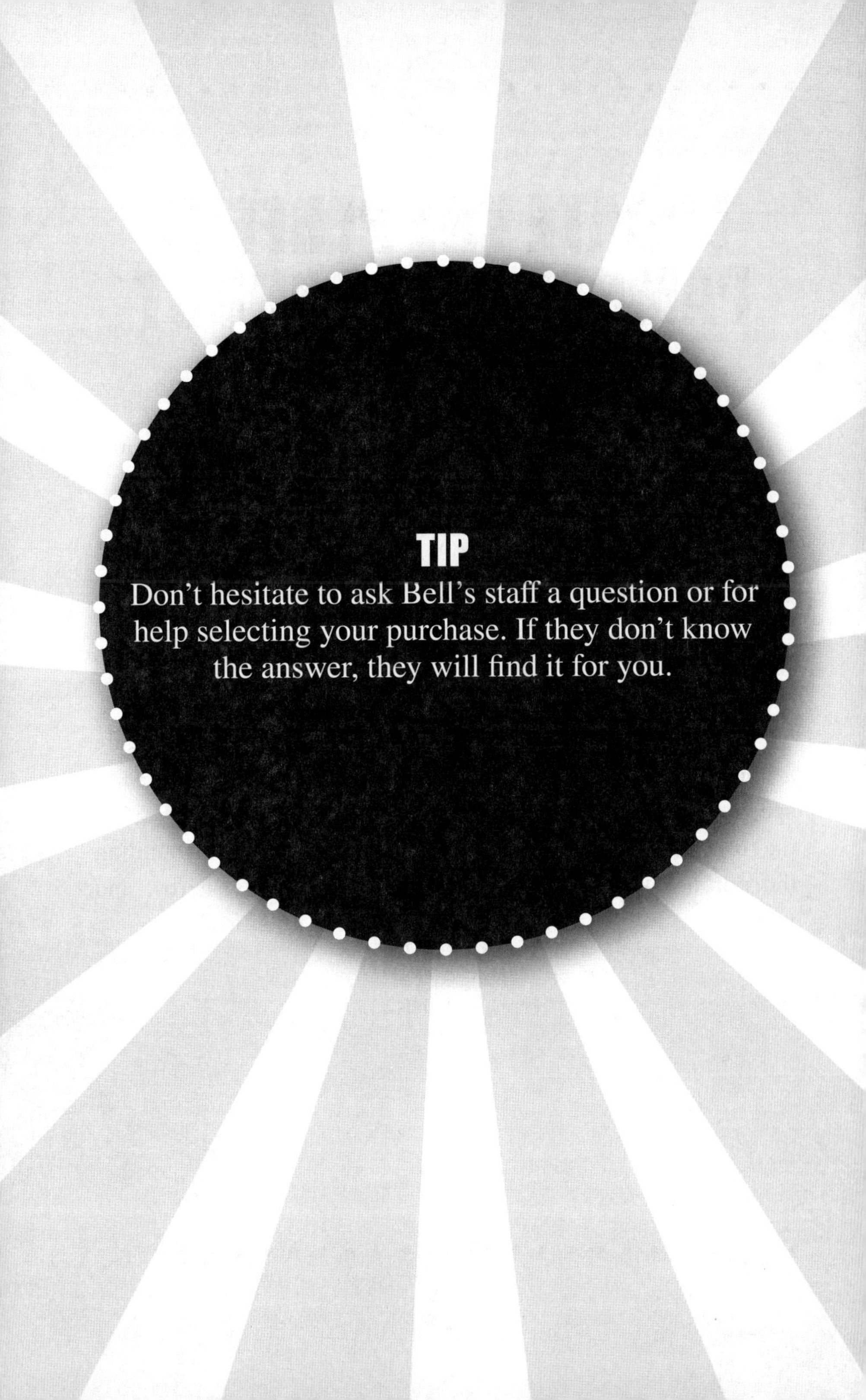
TIP
Don't hesitate to ask Bell's staff a question or for help selecting your purchase. If they don't know the answer, they will find it for you.

LOCATE THE PERFECT PAMPERING PRODUCT

AT CURATE ESSENTIALS

Located in a stately white 1914 home with a wraparound porch with twinkling lights and rocking chairs, Curate Essentials makes an impression before you even walk in the front door.

The herbal apothecary stocks pampering and health-care products, with nearly everything made on-site. You'll find all-natural soaps, balms, hand-painted and eco-friendly scarves, salt scrubs, herbal remedies, detergents, teas, jewelry, and decorative items.

When you're done shopping, don't miss stopping at the café at the front of the store. Order a pot of French-press coffee, a specialty tea, or a decadent coffee creation. Select a pastry, sit on the front porch, and enjoy the ambiance. The garden surrounding the porch is home to unusual and lovely plants, herbs, and vegetables, some of which are used in the store's products.

1302 Fort Bragg Rd., 910-920-4531
curateessentials.com

GET IT FRESH
AT DIRTBAG ALES FARMERS MARKET

From April through November, the place to be on Sunday is Dirtbag Ales in Hope Mills. Each Sunday they host the Dirtbag Ales Farmers Market. From 10 a.m. to 2 p.m., the field next to Dirtbag Ales is full of vendors selling their farm-fresh products and handmade creations.

Arrive early for a yoga class or to sip a Mimosa or a Bloody Mary at Dirty Whiskey Cocktail Bar while you shop the market. Walk the aisles of the market and choose from plants, vegetables, dairy products, jams and jellies, honey, craft items, and more.

Afterward, grab a table, sample a Dirtbag brew, and have a leisurely lunch from an on-site restaurant or that week's food trucks. Enjoy live music while the kids burn off energy at the playground and four-legged companions meet new friends at the dog park.

5435 Corporation Dr., Hope Mills, 910-426-2537
dirtbagales.com

CELEBRATE POP CULTURE
AT FAYETTEVILLE COMIC CON

Fayetteville Comic Con, an established, twice-annual pop culture convention, attracts a packed house to the Crown Complex each April and October.

Fayetteville's Comic Con represents the best in geek culture. The two-day con boasts a range of celebrity guests, authors, and comic book artists in artist alley. Vendors offer products inspired by comic books, science fiction, anime, horror, gaming, movies, wrestling, and other pop culture fandom.

The con is packed with celebrity panels, presentations, dance, and cosplay contests. Come dressed as your character and spend a few hours or the entire weekend. Fayetteville Comic Con is a shopper's paradise for anyone looking for the best in geek culture.

Tickets are available by the day or for the weekend. VIP and photo ops are sold in advance on the website.

1960 Coliseum Dr., 919-607-9199
fayettevillecomiccon.com

UNCOVER UNIQUE FINDS
AT PATE'S FARM MARKET

Pate's started as a farm stand when owner Mike Pate was in his teens. Later, he expanded into a farmers market. Today, Pate's is a full-scale grocery with fresh produce, hand-cut meats, a hot bar, and a massive nursery that is hopping year-round.

Plan to spend at least an hour discovering all that Pate's offers. After strolling the aisles, head outside to the nursery where you will undoubtedly get your daily step count in while you encounter seasonal offerings. The nursery is especially beautiful in the fall when it's packed with mums and pumpkins.

Head inside for lunch at the Deli's hot bar. The menu, which changes daily, often features southern staples such as chicken and pastry, fried chicken, macaroni and cheese, and ribs, in addition to vegetable and bean dishes.

6411 Raeford Rd., 910-426-1575
patesfarmmarket.com

LEAVE YOUR CARES BEHIND
AT FAYETTEVILLE WELLNESS CENTER

Fayetteville Wellness Center (FWC) provides an array of services, such as massage, cryotherapy, and compression therapy, but it's best known for offering float therapy. What is float therapy? Sometimes called a sensory deprivation chamber, a float tank has a bed of water that has been saturated with more than a thousand pounds of Epsom salt allowing users to float as effortlessly as they would at the Dead Sea. The lightproof and soundproof environment provides the ultimate in relaxation. An option allows selected music to be piped into the chamber.

No time for a float? Shop for fun and unique wellness products at the center's retail store in downtown Fayetteville. Epsom salts, jewelry, drinks, luxury chocolates, essential oils, soaps, and vitamins are among the picks at Fayetteville Wellness Center.

311 Hay St., 910-813-8129
shantiwellnessnc.com

TIP

Don’t miss Salt & Sage Apothecary products, FWC’s own bath and body line of scrubs, soaks, and salts.

100

STOCK YOUR PANTRY
AT APPLE CRATE NATURALS

Twenty-five years ago, when the Fayetteville-based owner of Apple Crate Naturals looked for natural foods and supplements, she had to travel at least 30 minutes out of town. She realized the Fayetteville community needed a natural market where they can find organic foods, supplements, and support for living a healthy life.

The Apple Crate was born in a tiny storefront in Hope Mills in 1997. Today, patrons regularly shop two locations. Each store offers a large refrigerated and frozen food section, shelf-stable foods, herbs, supplements, teas, aromatherapy, beauty products, and others. A wide range of selections are available in each category.

The all-natural merchandise at Apple Crate Naturals is either certified organic, non-GMO product verified, or independently researched by the friendly Apple Crate Naturals staff. No inhumane meats are sold, and all produce is 100 percent organic.

2711 Raeford Rd., 910-426-7777
5430 Camden Rd., 910-423-8800
applecratenaturals.com

Apple Crate Naturals, courtesy of Elizabeth Blevins

Courtesy of Stoney Point Trail of Terror

ACTIVITIES
BY SEASON

FALL

WINTER

SPRING

SUMMER

Cypress Lakes Golf Course,
courtesy of DistiNCtly Fayetteville

Napkins, courtesy of Tony Murnahan

SUGGESTED ITINERARIES

FOODIE FUN

THE PERFECT DATE

WEEKEND WARRIORS

FOR THE GUYS

CELEBRATE THE SEASON

FAMILY FUN

MILITARY AND HISTORY

GET OUTDOORS

EXPLORE THE ARTS

INDEX

Stop Button Bar, courtesy of Elizabeth Blevins